INVESTIGATING FIRST GRADE

Sunnyside Elementary School

Room 8

FACTS:

Thinking Kids®
Carson-Dellosa Publishing LLC
Greensboro, North Carolina

D1307199

Thinking Kids®
Carson-Dellosa Publishing LLC
P.O. Box 35665
Greensboro, NC 27425 USA

ISBN 978-1-4838-3496-2

CONTENTS

ABOUT THIS BOOK

In **Investigating First Grade**, your child will find hundreds of fun practice activities for essential math and language arts topics such as spelling words with long vowel sounds, adding and subtracting, writing sentences, and telling time. All practice activities support current state educational standards for your child's grade level. Spending just a few minutes each day with this book will help your son or daughter grow in confidence and master important skills that lead to success at school.

But **Investigating First Grade** is no ordinary workbook! It motivates students to learn with an intriguing mystery story to investigate and solve. While completing practice activities, your child will become a detective, collecting clues about suspects and answering vital questions about when, where, and how the mystery occurred. At the end of the book, your young investigator will put the clues together to crack the case!

Help your child follow these steps to become a first grade investigator:

1. **Read the Mystery Story: "Escape from Room Eight"**
    Read the mystery story beginning on page 6. Learn about where the mystery took place, what happened, and which suspects were witnessed at the scene. Look closely—you may find clues right in the story. Record clues in the **Detective's Notebook** on pages 202 and 203.

2. **Complete Learning Activities and Find Evidence**
    Complete skill-building math and language arts activities in each of four sections. On selected activity pages marked **Evidence Alert!**, solve puzzles to find evidence about the case. Keep track of the evidence you find. You will use it at the end of each section to discover a clue.

3. **Collect Clues**
    On the final page of each section, complete the **Clue Corner** activity. On this page, use all the evidence you found in the section to reveal a clue that answers a question such as

What? When? Where? How? or Who? Record each clue you find in the **Detective's Notebook** on pages 202 and 203.

4. **Record Clues in the Detective's Notebook**

    Each time you find a clue, record it in the **Detective's Notebook** on pages 202 and 203. Be sure to write clues exactly, one letter in each box shown. You will find clues to answer questions like these about the mystery: What happened? When did it happen? Where did it happen? How did it happen? and Who did it?

5. **Solve the Mystery**

    Use all the clues you collected to help complete the mystery story beginning on page 204. The letters you wrote inside green boxes in your **Detective's Notebook** will help you make choices. The choices you make will complete the story and solve the mystery. Congratulations, first grade investigator! You cracked the case and found clues about how to succeed at school, too!

Read the beginning of the mystery story. Then, follow the directions on page 8.

Escape from Room Eight

The job chart in room eight at Sunnyside Elementary School showed that Flynn Frunt was line leader for the week. On Monday, at lunch time, Flynn stood by the door. He waited for his classmates to clean up supplies and get in line. Finally, Ms. Minder nodded to Flynn, and he led the way through the hallways to the cafeteria.

When lunch and recess had ended, just after **one** o'clock in the afternoon, Flynn led the way back to room eight. Since he entered the classroom first, Flynn was first to see that Hattie was out of her cage. The fluffy gray hamster ran across the floor. Then, her little paws skittered to a stop. She sat up and looked at the kids with beady black eyes. Quickly, Ms. Minder picked up the class pet, placed her safely inside the cage on the table in the **science** center, and locked the latch tight. "How did Hattie get out?" Ms. Minder asked. No one had an answer.

On Tuesday, it happened again. Recess ended at one o'clock. A minute later, Flynn led his class toward room eight. As he turned a corner, Flynn saw Hattie dash out of the classroom and into the hallway. This time, the hamster did not stop. She ran straight toward the students. Kids shrieked as Hattie scampered between their feet. Finally, someone at the back of the line caught the little runner.

On Wednesday, Flynn led the line swiftly through the halls. When he opened the door to room eight, he saw something moving in the science center. There was Hattie climbing over a stack of batteries and racing around paper cups with leafy plants growing inside. She was just about to jump down from the table when Ms. Minder scooped her up.

The kids were worried about their pet. They loved Hattie and did not want her to be lost or hurt. Ms. Minder was the most worried of all. She called Flynn Frunt to her desk. "You are an extra-clever and extra-curious boy," she said. "Will you help solve this mystery? Can you find some clues about how our pet is getting out of her cage?"

"Yes, I will help!" promised Flynn. "I can start by talking to students who like to use the science center. Those kids are around Hattie's cage the most."

"Great idea!" exclaimed Ms. Minder. "Come back at the end of the day and let me know what you find out."

Flynn decided to talk to three classmates who visited the science center nearly every day.

First was G. Whiz. He loved all kinds of gadgets. At the science center, G. was trying to make a robot's arm move up and down.

Next was Pete Petty. He loved birds, reptiles, mammals, and creatures of all kinds. At the science center, Pete used books and websites to learn about animals.

Last was Joy Ride. She loved bikes, scooters, skateboards, and anything with wheels. At the science center, Joy was testing toy vehicles to see which ones rolled down a ramp the fastest.

Did one of these kids know how Hattie was escaping? It was time to find out.

G. WHIZ

JOY RIDE

PETE PETTY

It looks like this is a case for a first grade detective! How is Hattie the hamster getting out of her cage? Is someone letting her escape? Why? It is up to you to collect clues and solve the mystery.

Look again at the story. Can you find clues in **bold** that answer these questions: **When** did the hamster escape? and **Where** was the hamster cage? Write the clues in the **Detective's Notebook** on pages 202 and 203.

Now, keep going! Turn the page to complete learning activities, find evidence, collect clues, and solve the mystery.

TOP SECRET FILE #1:
Letters and Sounds

Learning Goals:

- Write all uppercase and lowercase alphabet letters
- Match uppercase and lowercase letters
- Spell consonant blends and digraphs
- Identify words with short vowel sounds and words with long vowel sounds
- Spell short and long vowel sounds
- Break words into syllables; understand that each syllable in a word has a vowel sound

Collect Evidence on These Evidence Alert! Pages:
Pages 21, 31, 43, 53

Use Evidence to Find a Clue on the Clue Corner Page:
Page 58

Clue Question:
How could Hattie escape from her cage?

Write Uppercase Letters

Write the uppercase letters.

Write Uppercase Letters

Write the uppercase letters.

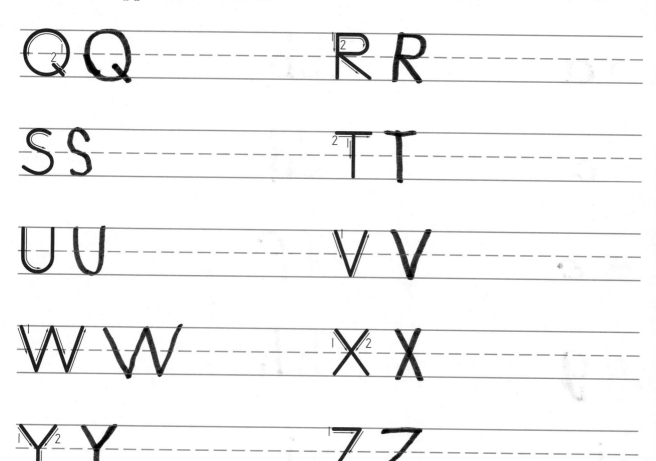

Q Q R R

S S T T

U U V V

W W X X

Y Y Z Z

Write Lowercase Letters

Write the lowercase letters.

a a   b b

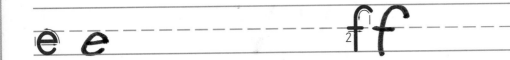

c c   d d

e e   f f

g g   h h

i i   j j

k k   l l

m m   n n

o o   p p

Name

Write Lowercase Letters

Write the lowercase letters.

q q   r r

s s   t t

u u   v v

w w   x x

y y   z z

Match Them Up

Draw lines to match the lowercase and uppercase letters.

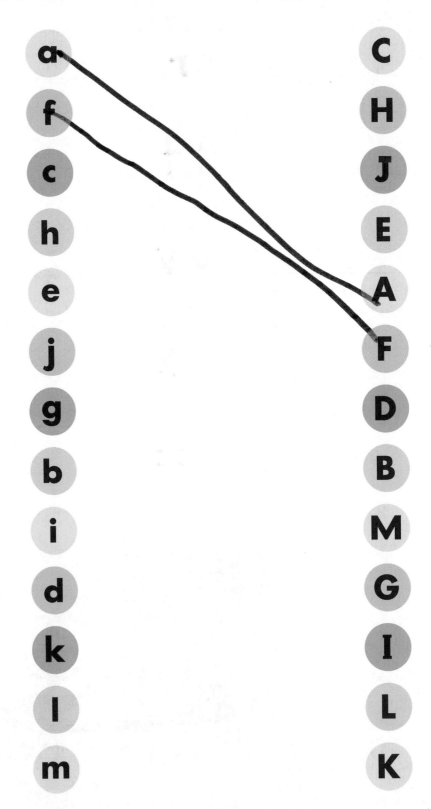

Match Them Up

Draw lines to match the lowercase and uppercase letters.

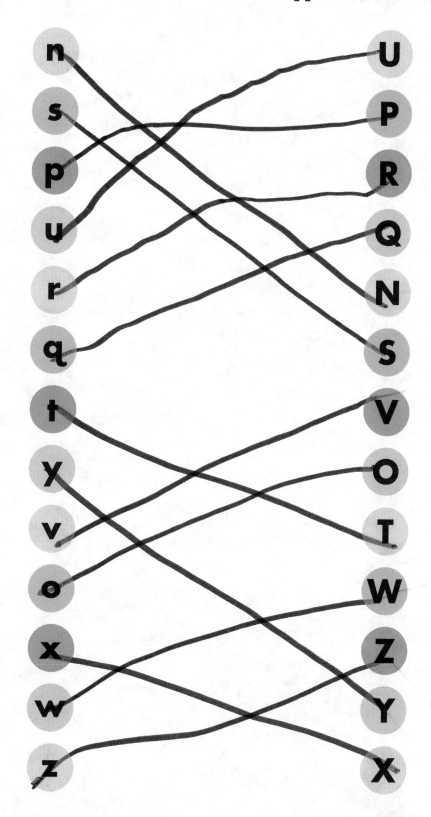

What Is Missing?

Write the missing lowercase or uppercase letter in each pair.

What Is Missing?

Write the missing lowercase or uppercase letter in each pair.

How Does It Begin?

Write the letter that makes the beginning sound for each picture name.

 g ift

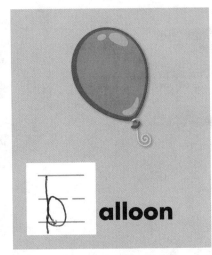 b alloon

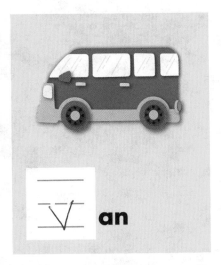 V an

 f ish

 d ice

 C at

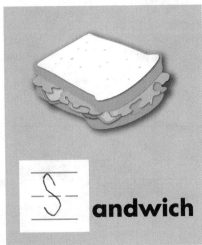 S andwich

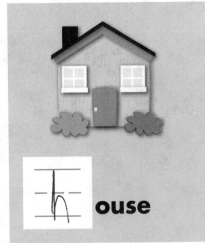 h ouse

 l ion

How Does It Begin?

Write the letter that makes the beginning sound for each picture name.

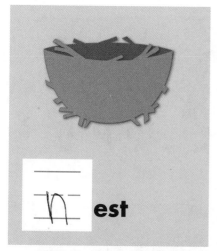

N est

Z ebra

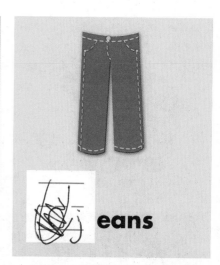

J eans

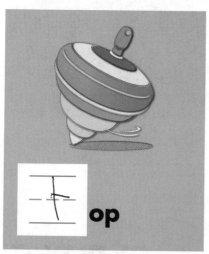

T op

Q ueen

r ice

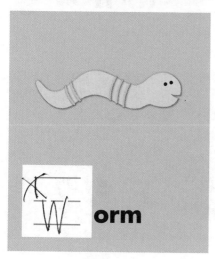

W orm

K ite

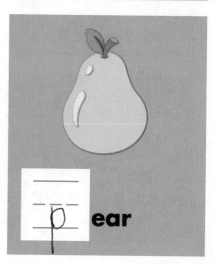

P ear

How Does It End?

Say the name of each picture. Circle the letter that makes the ending sound.

 **r s t x**

 **m p n t**

 **w g f t**

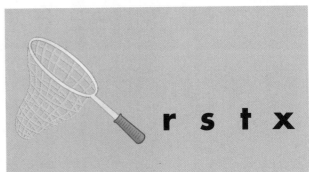 **r s t x**

 **r s t x**

 **m n w g**

 **r s t x**

 **p s n x**

Name

Letters Left Over

It is time to collect evidence about "Escape from Room Eight."

Flynn raced to the science center to get a closer look at Hattie's cage. Maybe she escaped all by herself, he thought. He began to inspect the cage carefully. The walls were metal bars. Under the soft bedding, the floor was made of hard plastic. Could Hattie slip through the edges where the walls and the floor met? To find out, use the letters to complete the words. Four letters will be left over.

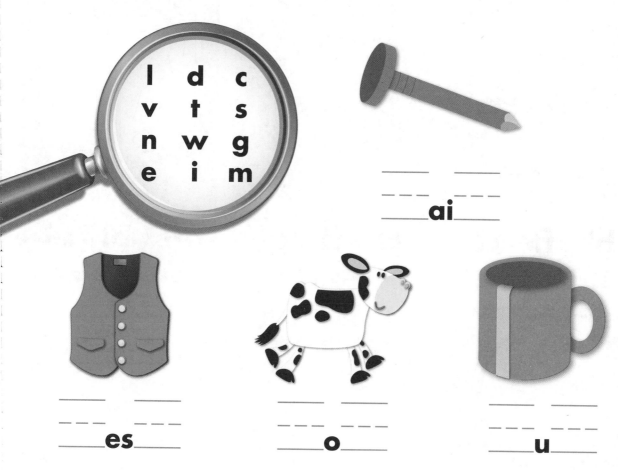

l d c
v t s
n w g
e i m

_____ ai _____

_____ es _____

_____ o _____

_____ u _____

Unscramble the letters you did not use to make a word that completes the sentence.

_____

Flynn found that each _____ of the cage was tight.

You found evidence! Use the word you wrote to help you find a clue on page 58.

Sounds That Blend

Consonant blends are two or more consonants whose sounds blend together in a word. Some consonant blends are made up of a consonant letter plus the letter **l**, as in **floor**. Say the name of each picture. Circle the consonant blend you hear at the beginning of the word. Color the pictures.

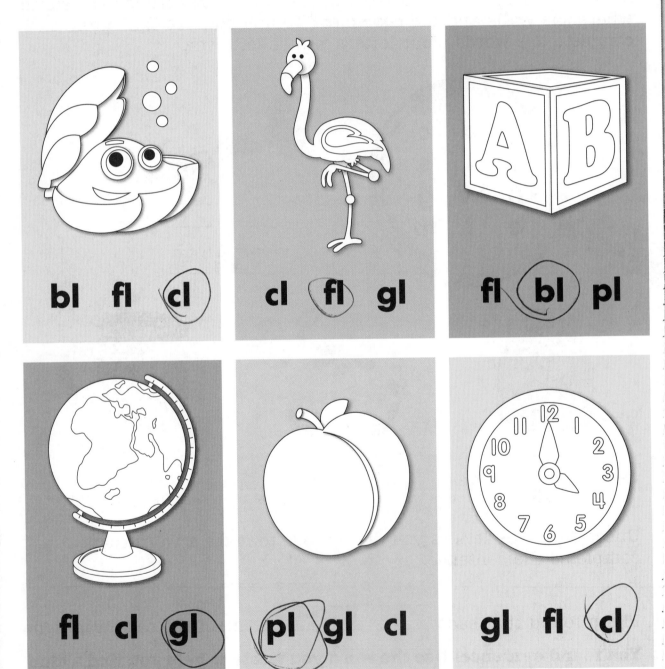

bl   fl   (cl)

cl   (fl)   gl

fl   (bl)   pl

fl   cl   (gl)

(pl)   gl   cl

gl   fl   (cl)

Name

Sounds That Blend

Some consonant blends are made up of a consonant letter plus the letter **r**, as in **brown**. Say the name of each picture. Write the consonant blend you hear at the beginning of the word. Color the pictures.

Blend It!

Say the name of each picture. Write the consonant blend you hear at the beginning of the word. Use these consonant blends: **bl**, **cr**, **cl**, **sl**. Color the pictures.

cr **ayon**

bl **anket**

cr **acker**

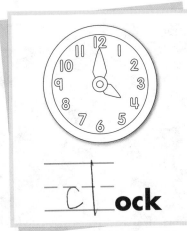

cl **ock**

bl **ock**

cl **oud**

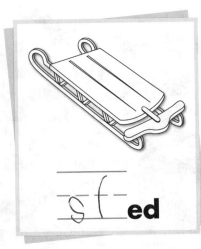

sl **ed**

cr **ab**

cl **am**

Blend It!

Say the name of each picture. Write the consonant blend you hear at the beginning of the word. Use these consonant blends: **br**, **fl**, **pl**, **sk**, **sn**.

They Begin with a Blend

Write a word that begins with a consonant blend to complete each sentence. Then, draw a picture to show each sentence.

sting	prize	drank	plant	stamp

Tom _____ his water.

A bee can _____ you.

I put a _____ on my letter.

The _____ is green.

My story won first _____.

Name _____

They End with a Blend

Write a word that ends with a consonant blend to complete each sentence. Then, draw a picture to show each sentence.

hand	mask	wild	melt	soft

I wore a scary _____.

The food is for _____ birds.

Please _____ cheese on my chips.

My teddy bear is _____.

Raise your _____ to answer.

Consonant Teams

In some words, two or three consonant letters form a consonant team that makes a single sound. Look at the consonant team at the beginning of each row. Then, say the name of each picture. Circle the picture that has the same consonant team.

wheel

wh

shoe

sh

chicken

ch

Name

Consonant Teams

Look at the consonant team at the beginning of each row. Then, say the name of each picture. Circle the picture that has the same consonant team.

duck

ck

ring

ng

tooth

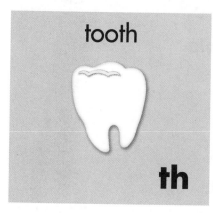

th

Go Consonant Team!

Write a word with a consonant team to complete each sentence.

shut	chain	patch	which	splash

My bike _____ is loose.

_____ sticker do you want?

Please _____ the door.

Use a _____ to cover the hole.

We like to _____ in the tub.

Catch the Code

It is time to collect more evidence about "Escape from Room Eight."

Flynn Frunt kept investigating. He grabbed a ruler, opened the cage, and gently lifted the warm little hamster to measure her. She was about two inches wide. Flynn set her back inside and latched the door. Then, he measured the space between the bars of the cage walls. Could Hattie squeeze through the space? To find out, complete the sentences with words from the box. Use the words to complete the code.

catch	ship	when

Did the _____ _____ sail?

You cannot _____ me!

_____ does the movie start?

Use the code to write a word that completes the sentence.

The space between the bars was too _____ for Hattie to squeeze through.

You found evidence! Use the word you wrote to help you find a clue on page 58.

The Sound of Short a

Short a is the middle sound in the word **rat**. Say the name of each picture. Then, spell each word by writing a consonant for the beginning sound, **a** for the **short a** sound in the middle, and a consonant for the ending sound. Color the pictures.

M a p

b a t

f a n

h a m

The Sound of Long a

Long a says its name. It is the vowel sound you hear in the word **same**. Say each word. Color the pictures for words that have the **long a** sound.

cake

frog

train

tree

grapes

crab

See It, Spell It

Write a **long a** word to name each picture. Notice different ways the **long a** sound can be spelled. Color the pictures.

apron   game   frame   pail   rake   table

Sound Sort

Read each word. The letters that spell the **short a** or **long a** sound are underlined. Write the word under the matching spelling pattern.

s<u>ay</u> w<u>eigh</u>	m<u>ai</u>l <u>a</u>lien	m<u>a</u>n sk<u>a</u>te	<u>a</u>t <u>a</u>corn	c<u>a</u>pe <u>eigh</u>t	w<u>ay</u> s<u>ai</u>l

short a spelled <u>a</u>

_____
_ _ _ _ _ _ _ _
_____
_____

long a spelled <u>ay</u>

_____
_ _ _ _ _ _ _ _
_____
_____

long a spelled <u>ai</u>

_____
_ _ _ _ _ _ _ _
_____
_____

long a spelled <u>a</u>

_____
_ _ _ _ _ _ _ _
_____
_____

long a spelled <u>ei</u>

_____
_ _ _ _ _ _ _ _
_____
_____

long a spelled <u>a-consonant-e</u>

_____
_ _ _ _ _ _ _ _
_____
_ _ _ _ _ _ _ _

The Sound of Short e

Short e is the middle sound in the word **get**. Say the name of each picture. Then, spell each word by writing a consonant for the beginning sound, **e** for the **short e** sound in the middle, and a consonant for the ending sound. Color the pictures.

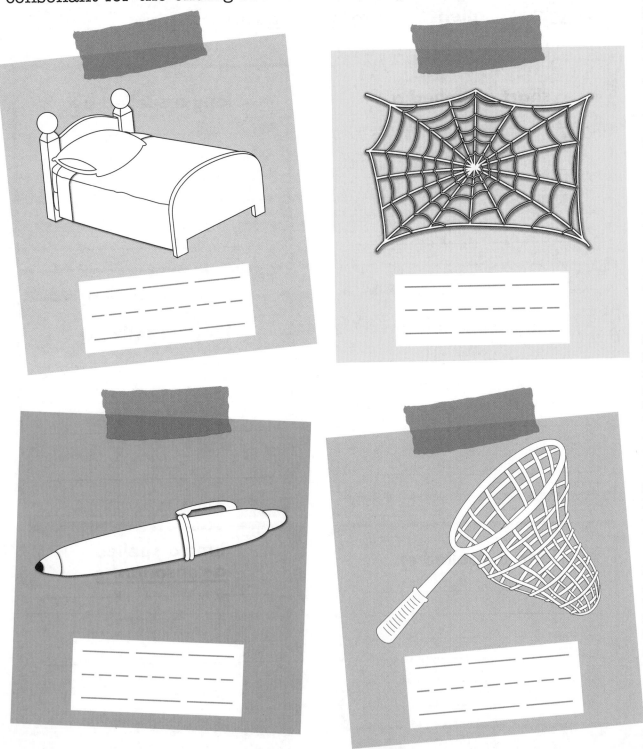

The Sound of Long e

Long e says its name. It is the vowel sound you hear in the word **seat**. Say each word. Color the pictures for words that have the **long e** sound.

feet

fish

tree

seal

tent

leaf

See It, Spell It

Write a **long e** word to name each picture. Notice different ways the **long e** sound can be spelled. Color the pictures.

| jellyfish | seal | key | queen | bee | beach |

_____

_____

_____

_____

_____

_____

Sound Sort

Read each word. The letters that spell the **short e** or **long e** sound are underlined. Write the word under the matching spelling pattern.

wh<u>e</u>n pl<u>ea</u>se	sorr<u>y</u> h<u>e</u>re	thr<u>ee</u> <u>e</u>gg	th<u>e</u>se bod<u>y</u>	gr<u>ee</u>n <u>ea</u>ch

short e spelled <u>e</u>

_____

_ _ _ _ _ _ _ _

_____

_ _ _ _ _ _ _ _

long e spelled <u>ee</u>

_____

_ _ _ _ _ _ _ _

_____

_ _ _ _ _ _ _ _

long e spelled <u>ea</u>

_____

_ _ _ _ _ _ _ _

_____

_ _ _ _ _ _ _ _

long e spelled <u>y</u>

_____

_ _ _ _ _ _ _ _

_____

_ _ _ _ _ _ _ _

long e spelled <u>e-consonant-e</u>

_____

_ _ _ _ _ _ _ _

_____

_ _ _ _ _ _ _ _

The Sound of Short i

Short i is the middle sound in the word **sit**. Say the name of each picture. Then, spell each word by writing a consonant for the beginning sound, **i** for the **short i** sound in the middle, and a consonant for the ending sound. Color the pictures.

The Sound of Long i

Long i says its name. It is the vowel sound you hear in the word **light**. Say each word. Color the pictures for words that have the **long i** sound.

kite

cake

ring

tie

pie

zipper

See It, Spell It

Write a **long i** word to name each picture. Notice different ways the **long i** sound can be spelled. Color the pictures.

five	pie	dinosaur	fire	slide	mice

_____

_____

_____

_____

_____

_____

Spelling Spy

Evidence ALERT!

It is time to collect more evidence about "Escape from Room Eight."

Flynn Frunt watched Hattie walk to the glass water bottle hanging on the side of the cage. Maybe, Flynn thought, Hattie could climb on top of the bottle and escape through the roof. Hattie drank from the bottle with her little pink tongue. Then, she stretched her front paws up the side of the bottle and tried to climb. What happened? To find out, write the **long i** word that matches each spelling clue.

invite	shy	pie	light

If you can spell dry, then you can spell _____ .

If you can spell night, then you can spell _____ .

If you can spell white, then you can spell _____ .

If you can spell tie, then you can spell _____ .

Now, write the first letter of each word you wrote, in order, to make a word that completes the sentence.

The smooth glass water bottle made Hattie's paws

____ ____ ____ ____
____ ____ ____ ____
____ ____ ____ ____ .

You found evidence! Use the word you wrote to help you find a clue on page 58.

The Sound of Short o

Short o is the middle sound in the word **got**. Say the name of each picture. Then, spell each word by writing a consonant for the beginning sound, **o** for the **short o** sound in the middle, and a consonant for the ending sound. Color the pictures.

The Sound of Long o

Long o says its name. It is the vowel sound you hear in the word **go**. Say each word. Color the pictures for words that have the **long o** sound.

goat

lock

yo-yo

deer

globe

coat

See It, Spell It

Write a **long o** word to name each picture. Notice different ways the **long o** sound can be spelled. Color the pictures.

globe	violin	boat	tomato	rope	snow

Sound Sort

Read each word. The letters that spell the **short o** or **long o** sound are underlined. Write the word under the matching spelling pattern.

| als<u>o</u> | w<u>oe</u> | b<u>ow</u> | n<u>o</u> | h<u>o</u>t | j<u>o</u>ke |
| m<u>o</u>p | n<u>o</u>se | s<u>oa</u>p | yell<u>ow</u> | r<u>oa</u>d | t<u>oe</u> |

short o spelled <u>o</u>
_____
_____
_____
_____

long o spelled <u>o</u>
_____
_____
_____
_____

long o spelled <u>ow</u>
_____
_____
_____
_____

long o spelled <u>oa</u>
_____
_____
_____
_____

long o spelled <u>oe</u>
_____
_____
_____
_____

long o spelled <u>o-consonant-e</u>
_____
_____
_____
_____

The Sound of Short u

Short u is the middle sound in the word **cup**. Say the name of each picture. Then, spell each word by writing a consonant for the beginning sound, **u** for the **short u** sound in the middle, and a consonant for the ending sound. Color the pictures.

t u b

S u n

r u g

B u s

The Sound of Long u

Long u says its name. It is the vowel sound you hear in the word **use**. Say each word. Color the pictures for words that have the **long u** sound.

cube

5 five

tube

music

plum

octopus

See It, Spell It

Write a **long u** word to name each picture. Notice different ways the **long u** sound can be spelled. Color the pictures.

unicycle	glue	cube	flute	tube	unicorn

Sound Sort

Read each word. The letters that spell the **short u** or **long u** sound are underlined. Write the word under the matching spelling pattern.

r<u>u</u>n	n<u>ew</u>	<u>u</u>s	<u>u</u>se	h<u>u</u>man
t<u>u</u>n<u>e</u>	st<u>u</u>dent	tr<u>ue</u>	f<u>ew</u>	resc<u>ue</u>

short u spelled <u>u</u>

long u spelled <u>u</u>

long u spelled <u>ue</u>

long u spelled <u>ew</u>

long u spelled <u>u-consonant-e</u>

Short or Long?

Read the name of each picture. Circle the pictures whose names have short vowel sounds. Draw a square around pictures whose names have long vowel sounds.

cheese

snake

goat

bib

dog

elephant

sun

dice

How Many Rhymes?

It is time to collect more evidence about "Escape from Room Eight."

Flynn Frunt had almost decided that Hattie's cage was escape-proof. He had just one more thought. Maybe Hattie could unlatch the door by herself. To test his idea, he held a hamster treat near the latch. The furry hamster came right over. She stretched her tiny arm through the bars to get the treat. Could Hattie reach the latch? To find out, write your own word that rhymes with each word shown.

bed

_____

gate

_____

lip

_____

boat

_____

seed

_____

tight

_____

Did you write more words with long vowel sounds or more words with short vowel sounds? Write **long** or **short** to answer the question and complete the sentence.

_____

The distance to the latch was too _____ for Hattie to reach.

You found evidence! Use the word you wrote to help you find a clue on page 58.

Spying Syllables

Read each word. Clap once for each syllable you hear. Write the number of syllables in the magnifying glass. If the word has more than one syllable, draw a line between the syllables. The first one is done for you.

kit|ten — 2

tree

sister

piano

phone

thunder

Spying Syllables

Read each word. Clap once for each syllable you hear. Write the number of syllables in the magnifying glass. If the word has more than one syllable, draw a line between the syllables.

flower

elephant

trash

blanket

hamster

Syllable Smash

Underline the letter or letters that spell the vowel sound in each syllable. Then, smash the syllables together and write the whole word in the blank.

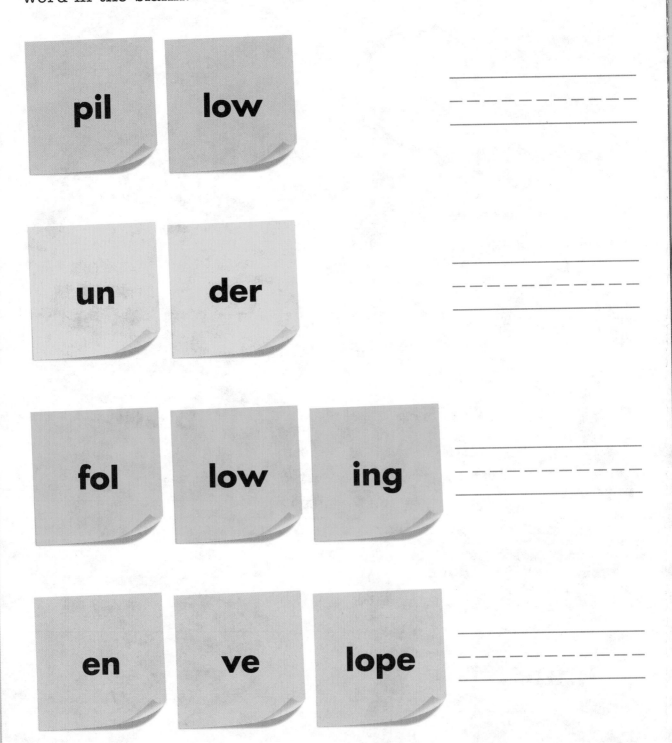

pil   low   _____

un   der   _____

fol   low   ing   _____

en   ve   lope   _____

Syllable Smash

Underline the letter or letters that spell the vowel sound in each syllable. Then, smash the syllables together and write the whole word in the blank.

to   **geth**   **er**   _____

home   **work**   _____

sev   **en**   **teen**   _____

help   **ful**   _____

Missing Syllables

It is time to find a clue about "Escape from Room Eight"!

Flynn Frunt gave Hattie the treat and petted her soft fur. He thought about his investigation so far. The walls, floor, and roof of the hamster cage were tight. So, how could Hattie escape? There was only one logical conclusion. What was it? To find out, write a word you collected as evidence on page 21, 31, 43, or 53 to complete a syllable in each word below.

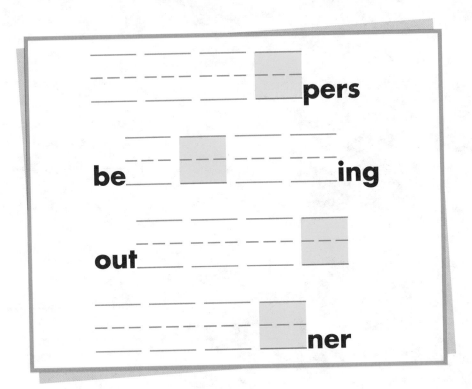

Now, unscramble the highlighted letters to write a word that finishes the sentence and forms a clue.

Clue: How could Hattie escape from her cage?

_____ _____ _____ _____
_____ _____ _____ _____ _____

Someone or something would have to _____ _____ _____ _____ the door from the outside.

Write the clue word you found in the Detective's Notebook on pages 202 and 203.

TOP SECRET FILE #2:
Addition and Subtraction

Learning Goals:

- Count to 120

- Understand that numbers 11–19 are formed from a ten and several ones

- Use a variety of strategies to add and subtract within 20

- Determine if addition and subtraction equations are true or false

- Find the unknown number in an addition or subtraction equation

- Use addition and subtraction to interpret data

- Use addition and subtraction to solve word problems

- Add multiples of 10

Collect Evidence on These Evidence Alert! Pages:
Pages 68, 76, 88, 98

Use Evidence to Find a Clue on the Clue Corner Page:
Page 106

Clue Question:
Who did it?

Suspect:
G. Whiz

Stack and Count

G. Whiz uses blocks to build and invent things. Draw more blocks in each stack. Begin with the number at the bottom of the stack. Write a number on each block you draw to count how many are in the stack.

18 +6

35 +10

76 +12

9 +5

111 +9

Stack and Count

Draw more blocks in each stack. Begin with the number at the bottom of the stack. Write a number on each block you draw to count how many are in the stack.

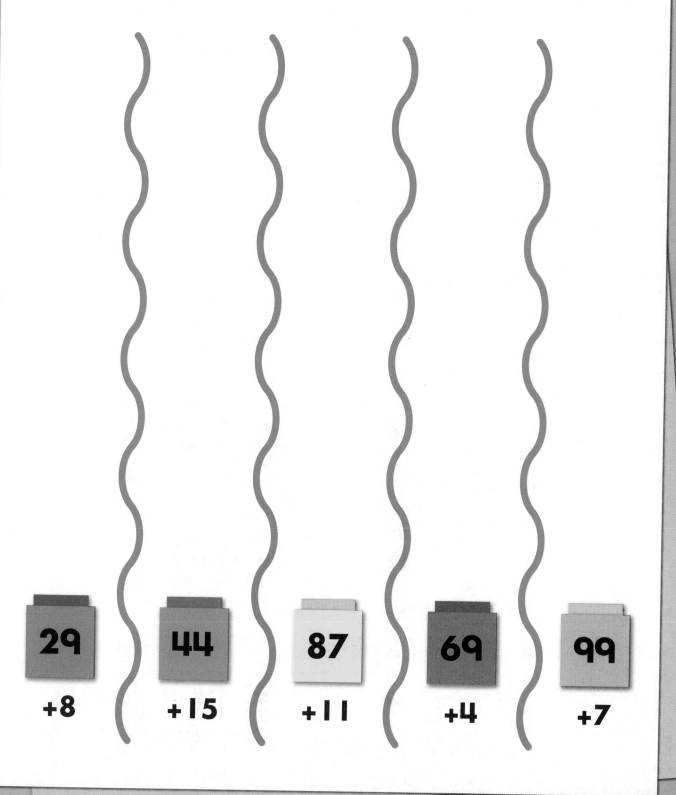

29
+8

44
+15

87
+11

69
+4

99
+7

Make 10

Use two different colors of crayons to color each ten frame in a different way. Show three different ways to make 10. Then, write an addition problem to match each frame.

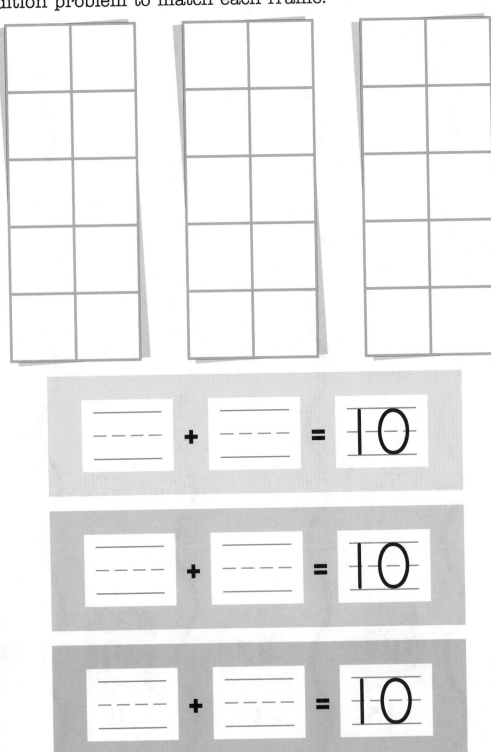

Make 10

Use two different colors of crayons to color each ten frame in a different way. Show three different ways to make 10. Then, write an addition problem to match each frame.

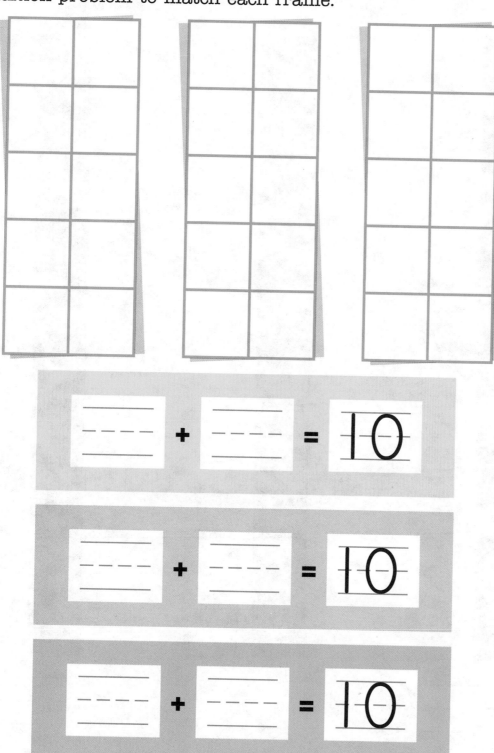

10 Plus Some

Add the yellow blocks to each stack of 10 red blocks. Write the sum.

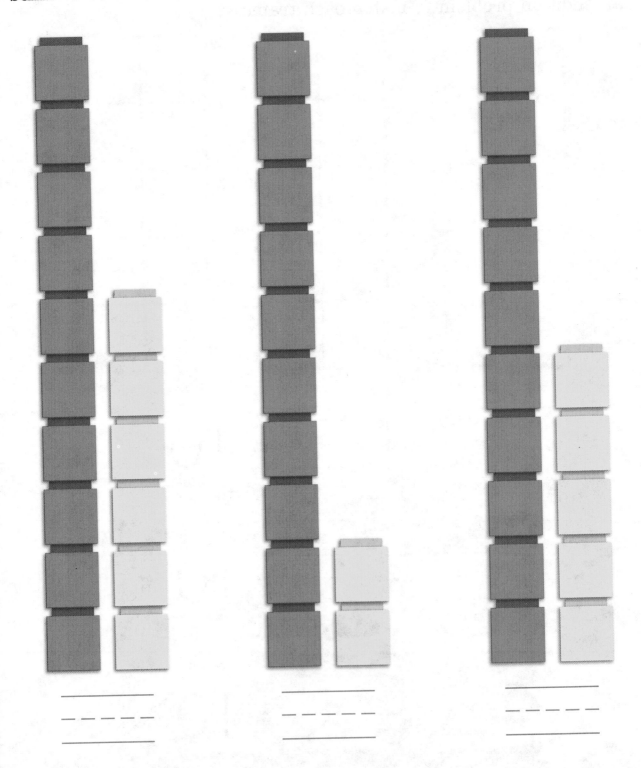

10 Plus Some

Add the green blocks to each stack of 10 red blocks. Write the sum.

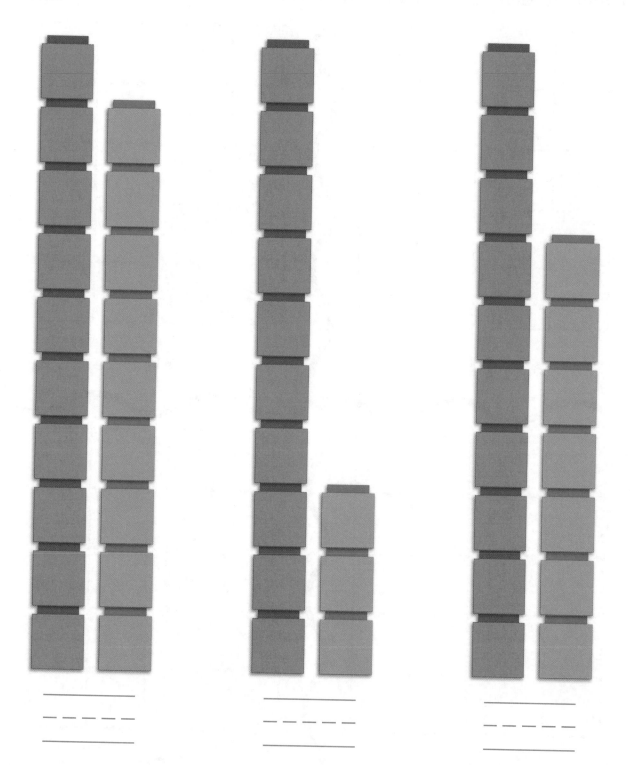

_____
_ _ _ _ _ _
_____

_____
_ _ _ _ _ _
_____

_____
_ _ _ _ _ _
_____

Frame Game

The first frame in each pair shows 10. Color boxes in the second frame in each pair to show the number.

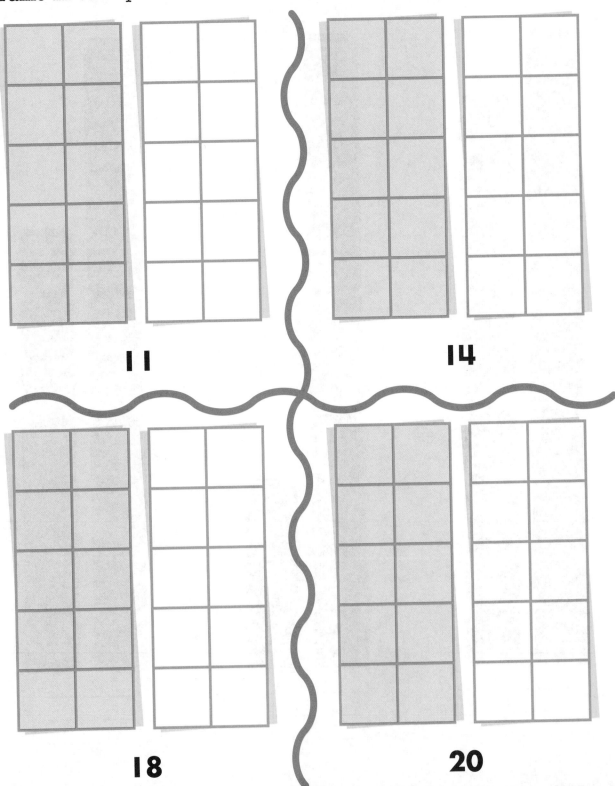

11

14

18

20

Another Frame Game

Write the missing numbers shown by the colored boxes. Solve the addition problems.

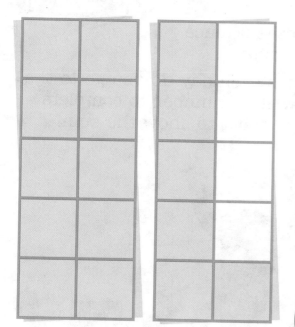

10 + 6 = 16

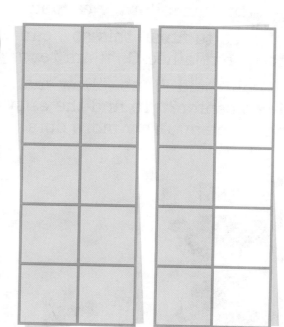

10 + 5 = 15

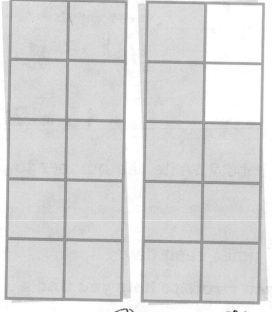

10 + 8 = 18

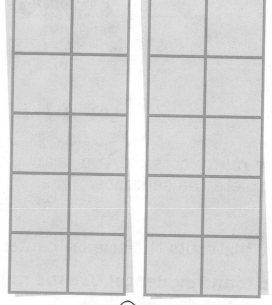

10 + 10 = 20

Dots on Robots

It is time to collect more evidence about "Escape from Room Eight."

Flynn found G. Whiz quickly reading a book in the classroom's library corner.

"I need to finish this so I can go to the science center," explained G. "I am testing my robot."

"Cool!" said Flynn. "How many times each day do you go to the science center?" To find the answer, write a number to complete each problem. Draw more dots on each robot to show the sum.

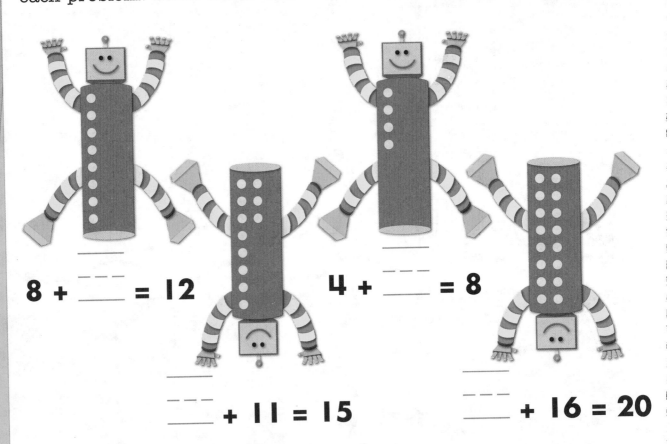

$8 +$ ___ $= 12$

$4 +$ ___ $= 8$

___ $+ 11 = 15$

___ $+ 16 = 20$

How many dots did you draw on each robot? Write the number to complete the sentence.

G. Whiz visits the science center ___ times each day.

You found evidence! Use the number you wrote to help you find a clue on page 106.

Click Ahead

Solve the addition problems. Put your finger on the number line at the place that matches the first number in each problem. Then, find the answer by counting forward the number of places shown by the second number in each problem.

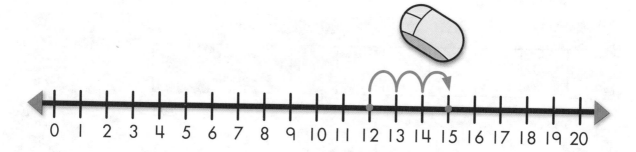

$12 + 3 =$ _____

Hint: From 12, count forward 3.

$8 + 4 =$ _____

Hint: From 8, count forward 4.

$6 + 9 =$ _____

Hint: From 6, count forward 9.

$10 + 5 =$ _____

Hint: From 10, count forward 5.

$3 + 14 =$ _____

Hint: From 3, count forward 14.

$7 + 0 =$ _____

Hint: From 7, count forward 0.

Color and Count

Use two different colors of crayons to color the blocks in each row.
Then, write numbers in the blanks to make two different addition
problems that match the blocks you colored. The first one is done
for you.

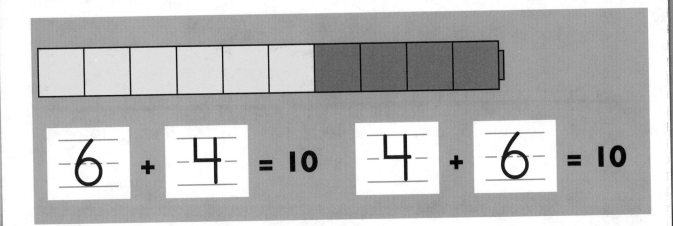

$6 + 4 = 10 \qquad 4 + 6 = 10$

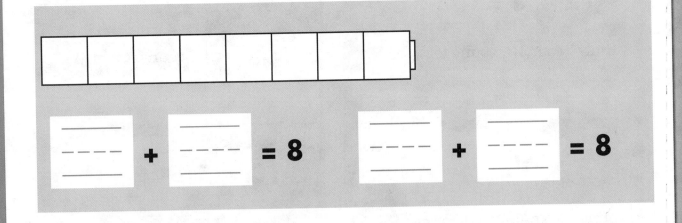

$\_\_ + \_\_ = 8 \qquad \_\_ + \_\_ = 8$

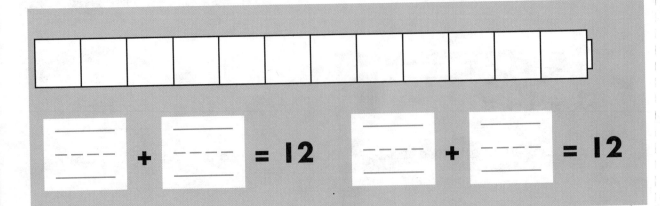

$\_\_ + \_\_ = 12 \qquad \_\_ + \_\_ = 12$

Color and Count

Use two different colors of crayons to color the blocks in each row. Then, write numbers in the blanks to make two different addition problems that match the blocks you colored.

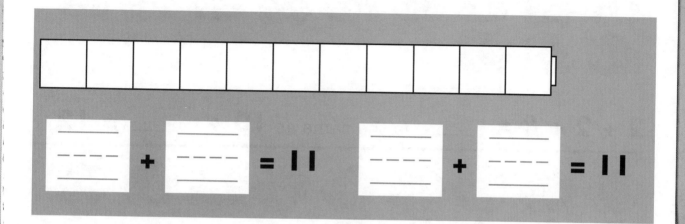

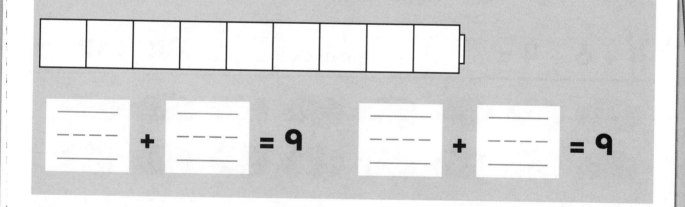

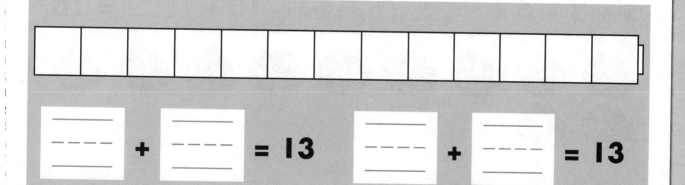

Rearranging Rocks (Making a Ten)

The science center in room eight has a rock collection. Circle 10 rocks in each group. Then, fill in the blanks to write different addition problems that have the same sum.

2 + 2 + 8 = _____ is the same as **10 +** _____ **= 12**

4 + 6 + 4 = _____ is the same as _____ **+ 4 = 14**

5 + 5 + 6 = _____ is the same as **10 +** _____ **= 16**

7 + 1 + 3 = _____ is the same as _____ **+ 1 = 11**

Name

Rearranging Rocks (Making Doubles)

Fill in the blanks to write different addition problems that have the same sum. Count the rocks to help you.

7 + 8 = _____ is the same as **7 + 7 +** _____ **= 15**

6 + 7 = _____ is the same as **6 +** _____ **+ 1 = 13**

8 + 9 = _____ is the same as **8 + 8 +** _____ **= 17**

5 + 6 = _____ is the same as **5 +** _____ **+ 1 = 11**

Add Two Together

Write each sum on a magnifying glass.

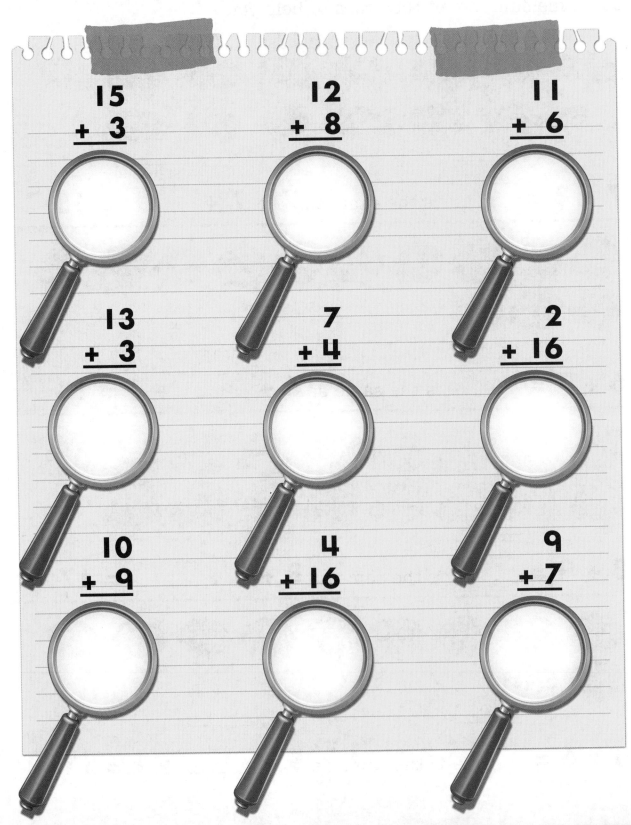

15
+ 3

12
+ 8

11
+ 6

13
+ 3

7
+ 4

2
+ 16

10
+ 9

4
+ 16

9
+ 7

Add Three Together

Write each sum on a magnifying glass. Look for ways to make 10 or add doubles.

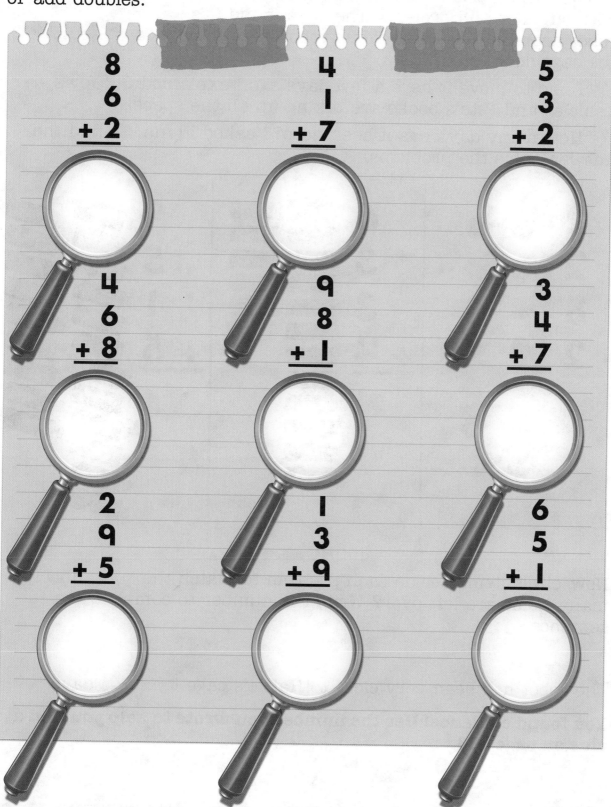

$$\begin{array}{r} 8 \\ 6 \\ + 2 \\ \hline \end{array}$$

$$\begin{array}{r} 4 \\ 1 \\ + 7 \\ \hline \end{array}$$

$$\begin{array}{r} 5 \\ 3 \\ + 2 \\ \hline \end{array}$$

$$\begin{array}{r} 4 \\ 6 \\ + 8 \\ \hline \end{array}$$

$$\begin{array}{r} 9 \\ 8 \\ + 1 \\ \hline \end{array}$$

$$\begin{array}{r} 3 \\ 4 \\ + 7 \\ \hline \end{array}$$

$$\begin{array}{r} 2 \\ 9 \\ + 5 \\ \hline \end{array}$$

$$\begin{array}{r} 1 \\ 3 \\ + 9 \\ \hline \end{array}$$

$$\begin{array}{r} 6 \\ 5 \\ + 1 \\ \hline \end{array}$$

Spare Parts

It is time to collect more evidence about "Escape from Room Eight."

The table in the science center was crowded with supplies and projects. The boys found G.'s robot near Hattie's cage. "Your robot is very close to the cage door," said Flynn.

"I had to move it here a few days ago," explained G. "Joy's vehicles and Pete's books are taking up all the space!"

"How many days has it been here?" asked Flynn. To find the answer, solve the problems.

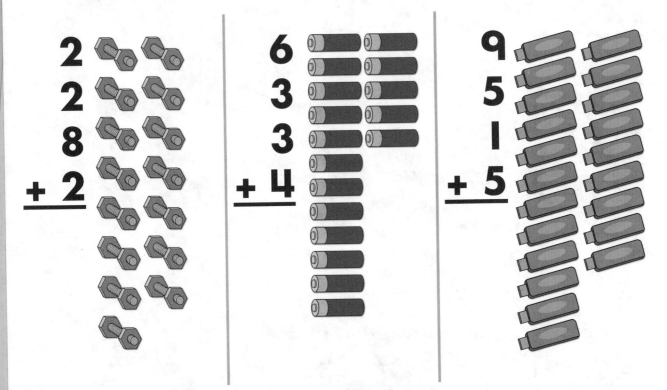

$$\begin{array}{r} 2 \\ 2 \\ 8 \\ +\ 2 \\ \hline \end{array} \qquad \begin{array}{r} 6 \\ 3 \\ 3 \\ +\ 4 \\ \hline \end{array} \qquad \begin{array}{r} 9 \\ 5 \\ 1 \\ +\ 5 \\ \hline \end{array}$$

Now, circle items beside each problem to match the sum. How many items are left over? Write the number to complete the sentence.

_____
_ _ _

The robot had been very close to Hattie's cage for _____ days.

You found evidence! Use the number you wrote to help you find a clue on page 106.

Take Some Away

Subtracting is taking some away. Solve the subtraction problems.
Cross out the pictures you are taking away.

_____

8 – 3 = _____

_____

10 – 6 = _____

_____

13 – 9 = _____

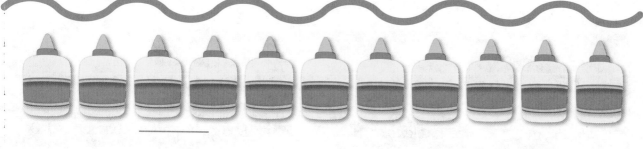

_____

11 – 5 = _____

Click Back

Solve the subtraction problems. Put your finger on the number line at the place that matches the first number in each problem. Then, find the answer by counting backward the number of places shown by the second number in each problem.

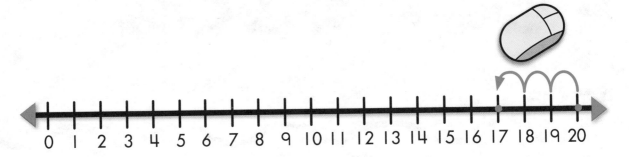

20 – 3 = ____

Hint: From 20, count backward 3.

9 – 3 = ____

Hint: From 9, count backward 3.

15 – 8 = ____

Hint: From 15, count backward 8.

20 – 11 = ____

Hint: From 20, count backward 11.

17 – 5 = ____

Hint: From 17, count backward 5.

15 – 0 = ____

Hint: From 15, count backward 0.

Click Back

Solve the subtraction problems. Put your finger on the number line at the place that matches the first number in each problem. Then, find the answer by counting backward the number of places shown by the second number in each problem.

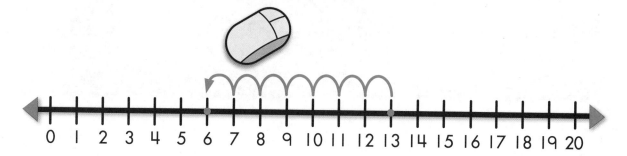

13 − 7 = ____

Hint: From 13, count backward 7.

20 − 10 = ____

Hint: From 20, count backward 10.

8 − 1 = ____

Hint: From 8, count backward 1.

15 − 6 = ____

Hint: From 15, count backward 6.

17 − 11 = ____

Hint: From 17, count backward 11.

12 − 8 = ____

Hint: From 12, count backward 8.

Thinking Machine

First, solve each addition problem. Use the sum to help you solve the subtraction problem.

$18 - 9 =$ _____   THINK $9 +$ _____ $= 18$

$14 - 6 =$ _____   THINK $6 +$ _____ $= 14$

$17 - 8 =$ _____   THINK $8 +$ _____ $= 17$

$15 - 7 =$ _____   THINK $7 +$ _____ $= 15$

Thinking Machine

First, solve each addition problem. Use the sum to help you solve the subtraction problem.

$18 - 8 =$ ___ THINK $8 +$ ___ $= 18$

$14 - 5 =$ ___ THINK $5 +$ ___ $= 14$

$17 - 6 =$ ___ THINK $6 +$ ___ $= 17$

$15 - 4 =$ ___ THINK $4 +$ ___ $= 15$

Subtraction Squares

Subtract each row and then each column. Write the answers on the lines.

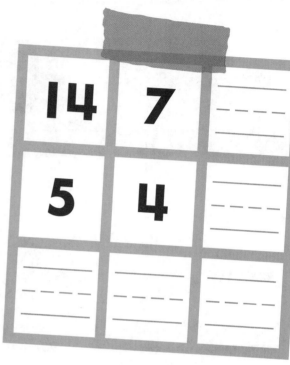

Subtraction Squares

Subtract each row and then each column. Write the answers on the lines.

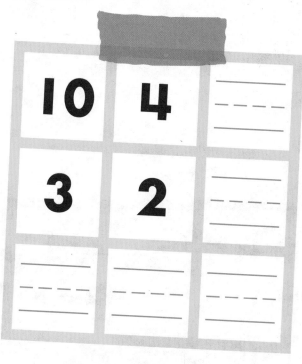

10	4	___
3	2	___
___	___	___

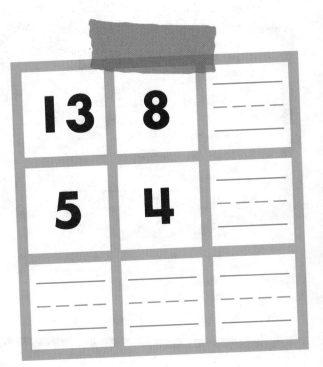

13	8	___
5	4	___
___	___	___

15	7	___
9	4	___
___	___	___

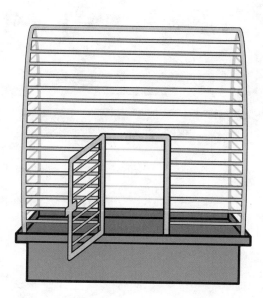

Subtraction Screens

Fill in the blanks to write subtraction problems that have the same difference.

$12 - \underline{\hspace{1cm}} = 9$

$\underline{\hspace{1cm}} - 2 - 1 = 9$

$10 - 1 = \underline{\hspace{1cm}}$

$17 - 9 = \underline{\hspace{1cm}}$

$17 - \underline{\hspace{1cm}} - 2 = 8$

$10 - 2 = \underline{\hspace{1cm}}$

$15 - \underline{\hspace{1cm}} = 9$

$15 - \underline{\hspace{1cm}} - 1 = 9$

$10 - \underline{\hspace{1cm}} = 9$

$13 - 5 = \underline{\hspace{1cm}}$

$13 - 3 - \underline{\hspace{1cm}} = 8$

$10 - 2 = \underline{\hspace{1cm}}$

Subtraction Screens

Fill in the blanks to write subtraction problems that have the same difference.

$14 - 8 =$ _____

$14 - 4 -$ _____ $= 6$

$10 -$ _____ $= 6$

$11 - 2 =$ _9_

_____ $- 1 - 1 = 9$

$10 -$ _____ $= 9$

$16 - 7 =$ _____

$16 -$ _____ $- 1 = 9$

_____ $- 1 = 9$

$18 -$ _____ $= 9$

$18 - 8 -$ _____ $= 9$

$10 - 1 =$ _____

Subtract

Write each difference on a magnifying glass.

$$\begin{array}{r} 20 \\ -\ 3 \\ \hline \end{array}$$

$$\begin{array}{r} 12 \\ -\ 8 \\ \hline \end{array}$$

$$\begin{array}{r} 16 \\ -\ 7 \\ \hline \end{array}$$

$$\begin{array}{r} 20 \\ -\ 5 \\ \hline \end{array}$$

$$\begin{array}{r} 14 \\ -\ 3 \\ \hline \end{array}$$

$$\begin{array}{r} 11 \\ -\ 6 \\ \hline \end{array}$$

$$\begin{array}{r} 13 \\ -\ 10 \\ \hline \end{array}$$

$$\begin{array}{r} 15 \\ -\ 9 \\ \hline \end{array}$$

$$\begin{array}{r} 18 \\ -\ 9 \\ \hline \end{array}$$

Name

Subtract

Write each difference on a magnifying glass.

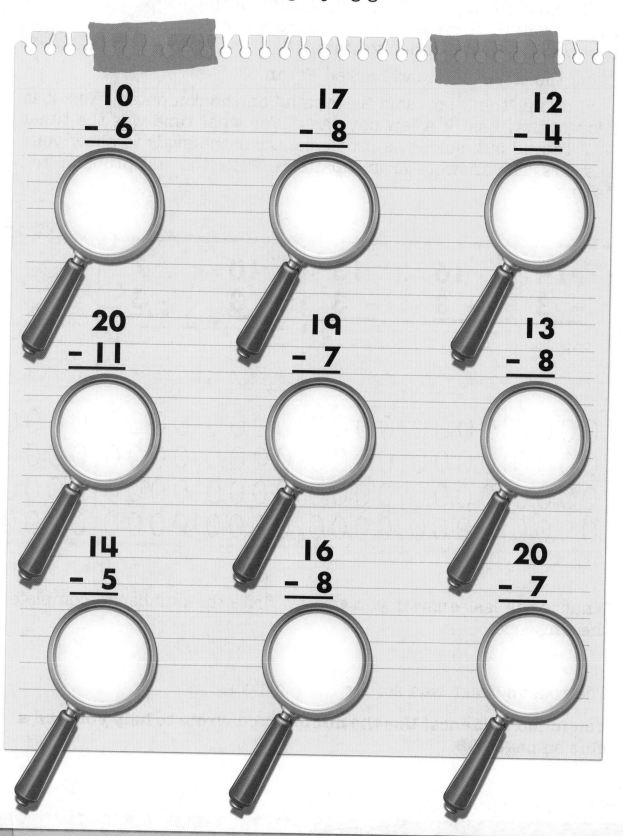

$$10 - 6$$

$$17 - 8$$

$$12 - 4$$

$$20 - 11$$

$$19 - 7$$

$$13 - 8$$

$$14 - 5$$

$$16 - 8$$

$$20 - 7$$

Time for a Pattern

Evidence ALERT!

It is time to collect more evidence about "Escape from Room Eight."

"I wrote a computer program to control the robot," said G. "I press a button to start the program, or I set a timer to start it."

"Is the timer set now?" asked Flynn.

"I do not think so," said G., tapping on the computer. "Yes, it is! I forgot that I set it a few days ago." For what time was the timer set? To find out, solve the problems. Color the ovals to show your answers. The answers form a pattern. Write the last problem and its answer.

19 − 3	16 − 3	13 − 3	10 − 3	7 − 3	
0 0 0 0 0 0 0 0 0 0 0 0 0 0 0 0	0 0 0 0 0 0 0 0 0 0 0 0 0 0 0 0	0 0 0 0 0 0 0 0 0 0 0 0 0 0 0 0	0 0 0 0 0 0 0 0 0 0 0 0 0 0 0 0	0 0 0 0 0 0 0 0 0 0 0 0 0 0 0 0	0 0 0 0 0 0 0 0 0 0 0 0 0 0 0 0

What is the last answer you wrote? Write the number to complete the sentence.

_____

The robot's timer was set for _____ o'clock.

You found evidence! Use the number you wrote to help you find a clue on page 106.

Fact Families

Write four facts for each fact family.

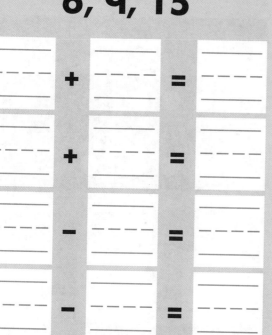

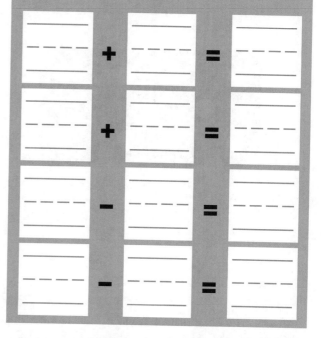

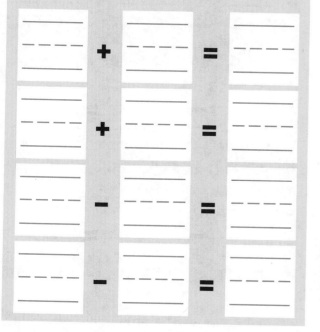

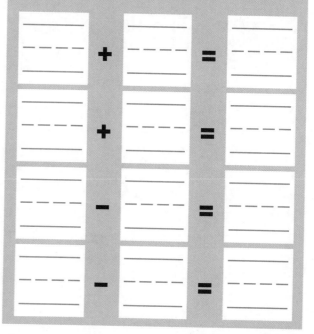

Seeing Spots

Use the numbers shown by the dots on the dominoes to write four facts for each fact family.

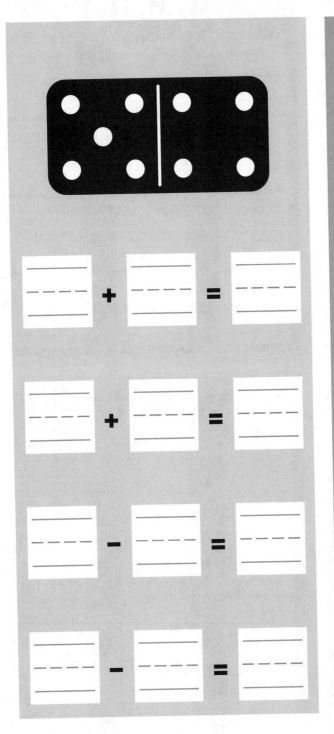

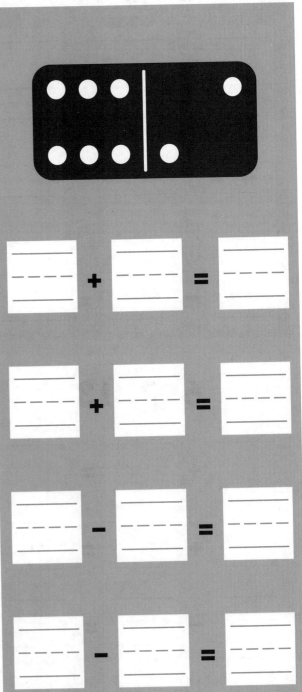

Seeing Spots

Use the numbers shown by the dots on the dominoes to write four facts for each fact family.

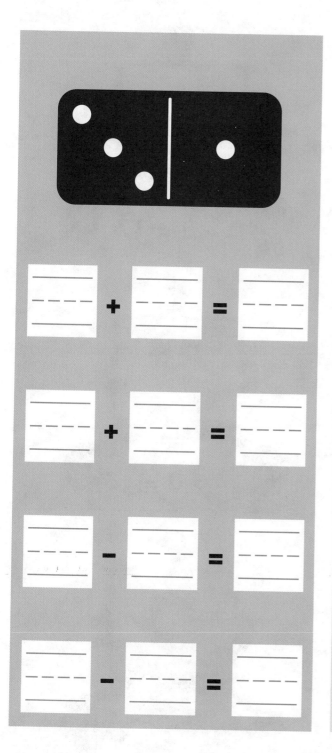

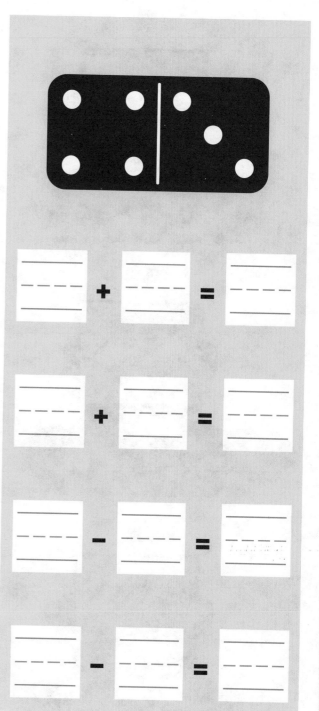

True or False?

Circle each equation that is true and draw a smile on the robot's face. Cross out each equation that is false and draw a frown on the robot's face.

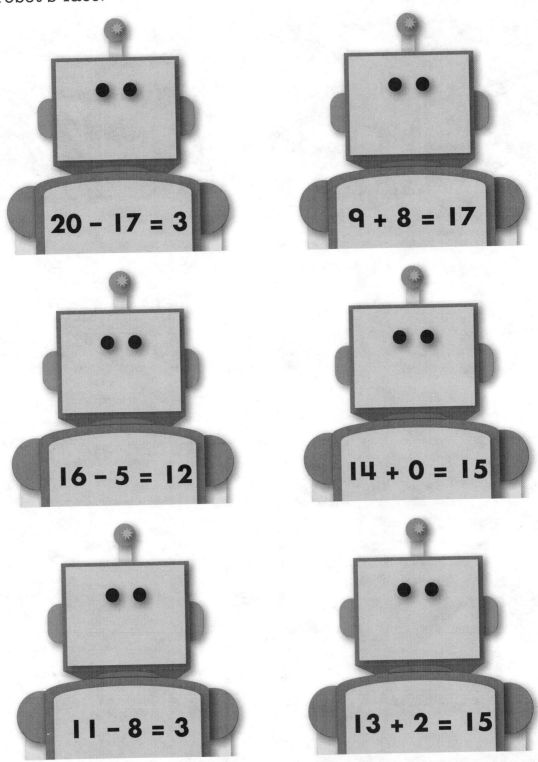

20 – 17 = 3

9 + 8 = 17

16 – 5 = 12

14 + 0 = 15

11 – 8 = 3

13 + 2 = 15

True or False?

Circle each equation that is true and draw a smile on the robot's face. Cross out each equation that is false and draw a frown on the robot's face.

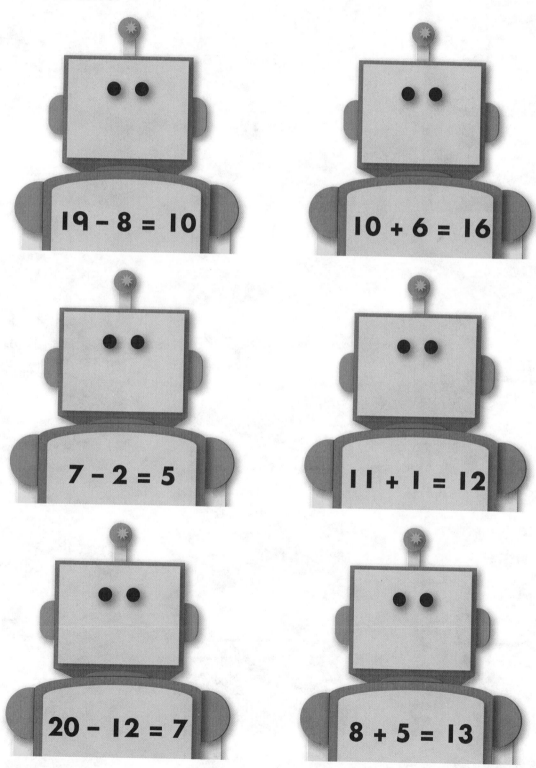

$19 - 8 = 10$

$10 + 6 = 16$

$7 - 2 = 5$

$11 + 1 = 12$

$20 - 12 = 7$

$8 + 5 = 13$

What Is Missing?

Write the number that makes each equation true.

$$15 + \square = 18$$

$$\square - 7 = 4$$

$$18 + 2 = \square$$

$$6 + \square = 13$$

$$\square - 0 = 8$$

$$13 + 5 = \square$$

$$\square - 9 = 6$$

$$12 + \square = 20$$

$$20 - 9 = \square$$

Graph It!

Count and graph items found in the science center. Start at the bottom of each column. Color one space for each item you count.

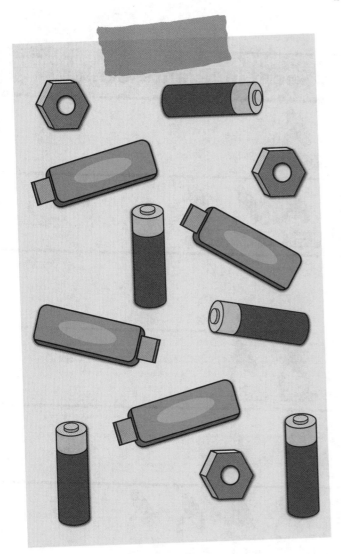

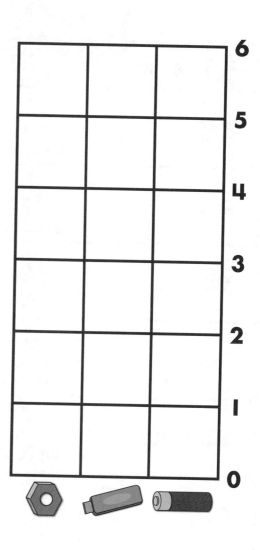

How many batteries are shown? _____

How many items in all are shown? _____

How many more batteries than nuts are shown? _____

Science Center Students

Ms. Minder made a picture graph to show how much time students in room eight spent in the science center during one week.

Student	Hours Spent in Science Center
Raj	🔬 🔬 🔬
Joy	🔬 🔬 🔬 🔬 🔬
Tasha	🔬
Pete	🔬 🔬 🔬 🔬
Hannah	🔬 🔬
G.	🔬 🔬 🔬 🔬 🔬 🔬
Thanvi	🔬 🔬
Daniel	🔬 🔬 🔬 🔬

 = one hour spent in science center

Use the graph on page 96 to answer the questions.

1. How many students spent time in the science center during the week?

   _ _ _ _

   _____ students

2. Who spent the most time in the science center?

   _ _ _ _ _ _ _ _ _ _ _ _ _ _ _

   _____

3. Who spent the least time in the science center?

   _ _ _ _ _ _ _ _ _ _ _ _ _ _

   _____

4. How many students spent two hours in the science center during the week?

   _ _ _ _

   _____ students

5. How many more hours did Joy spend in the science center than Thanvi?

   _ _ _ _

   _____ hours

6. How many hours did Raj and Daniel spend in the science center?

   _ _ _ _

   _____ hours

7. How many hours did Tasha, Pete, and Hannah spend in the science center?

   _ _ _ _

   _____ hours

8. How many hours were spent in the science center altogether?

   _ _ _ _

   _____ hours

Computer Time

It is time to collect more evidence about "Escape from Room Eight."

"A number 1 in the program tells the robot to raise its arm," explained G.

"Does another number tell the robot to lower its arm?" asked Flynn.

"Correct!" exclaimed G. What number tells the robot to lower its arm? To find out, complete the graph by writing the total number of students who signed up for computer time each week. For now, ignore the question marks.

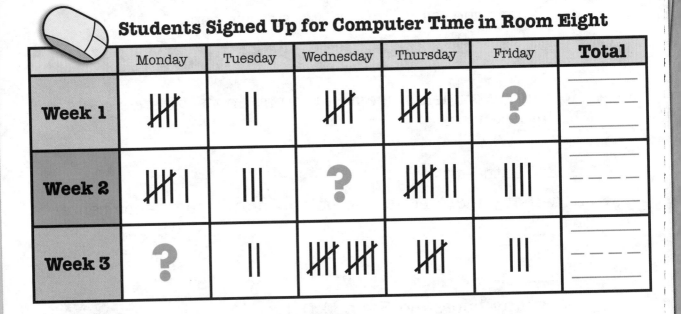

Students Signed Up for Computer Time in Room Eight

	Monday	Tuesday	Wednesday	Thursday	Friday	**Total**
Week 1	卌	||	卌	卌 |||	?	_____
Week 2	卌		|||	?	卌 ||	||||	_____
Week 3	?	||	卌 卌	卌	|||	_____

Each week, 20 students may sign up for computer time in room eight. How many students could sign up for computer time on the days with a question mark? Write the number to complete the sentence.

_____

In G.'s computer program, the number _____ tells the robot to lower its arm.

You found evidence! Use the number you wrote to help you find a clue on page 106.

Name

In Room Eight

Write the number that solves each story problem.

A rack in the science center holds 16 pairs of scissors. Students are using 11 pairs of scissors. How many pairs of scissors are still on the rack?

```
- - - - -
```
pairs of scissors

Sunnyside Elementary School has 3 floors. There are 6 classrooms on the first floor, 8 classrooms on the second floor, and 5 classrooms on the third floor. How many classrooms are there at Sunnyside?

```
- - - - -
```
classrooms

On Monday morning, 9 students said "Hi" to Hattie. On Monday afternoon, 6 different students said "Hi" to Hattie. How many students greeted Hattie that Monday?

```
- - - - -
```
students

The science center has space for 12 students. 7 students are working there now. How many more students can work in the science center?

```
- - - - -
```
students

Draw and Solve

Draw pictures to match each story problem. Then, solve the problem and write the answer.

There are 20 students in room eight. 14 are already in line to go to lunch. How many students are still cleaning up?

_____
_ _ _ _ _
_____ students

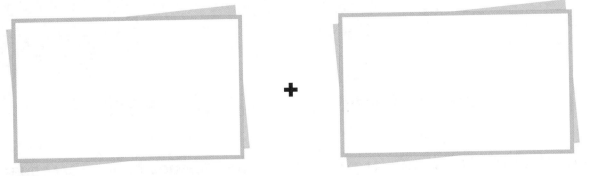

Hattie the hamster ate 6 treats on Thursday and 8 treats on Friday. How many treats did she eat altogether?

_____
_ _ _ _ _
_____ treats

G. tested his robot's arm 17 times. It worked perfectly 8 times. How many times did it not work?

_____
_ _ _ _ _
_____ times

Draw and Solve

Draw pictures to match each story problem. Then, solve the problem and write the answer.

[ ] − [ ]

Room eight will hold a science fair on March 19. If today is March 5, how many days are left before the science fair?

_____
_ _ _ _
_____ days

[ ] + [ ] + [ ]

G. Whiz's robot kit has 6 wheels, 4 cables, and 2 claws. How many parts does it have in all?

_____
_ _ _ _
_____ parts

[ ] + [ ]

Hattie climbed in and out of her tube for 8 minutes. Then, she ran on her wheel for 8 minutes. For how many minutes in all did she play?

_____
_ _ _ _
_____ minutes

Count Tens

Each stack is made from 10 blocks. Count the stacks. Write a number that ends with 0 to show how many are in each group.

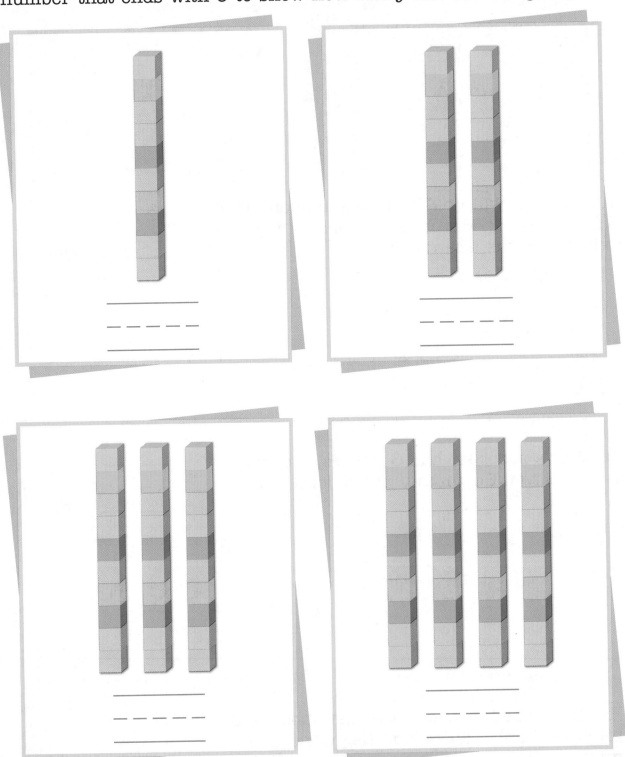

Count Tens

Each stack is made from 10 blocks. Count the stacks. Write a number that ends with 0 to show how many are in each group.

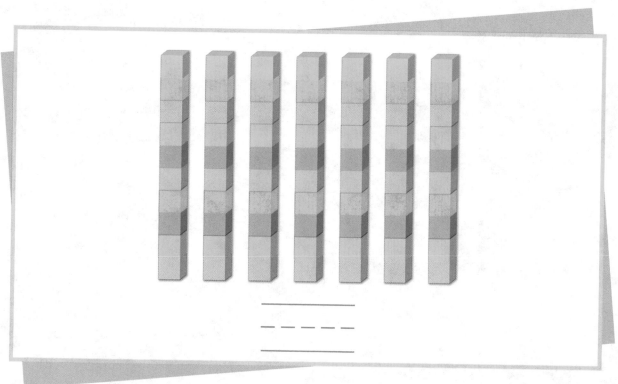

Count Tens

Each stack is made from 10 blocks. Count the stacks. Write a number that ends with 0 to show how many are in each group.

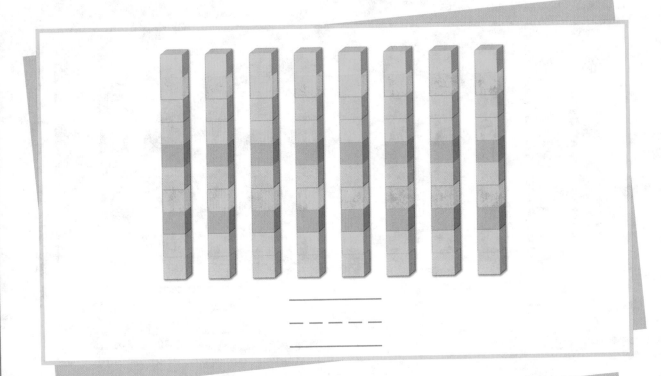

_ _ _ _ _ _

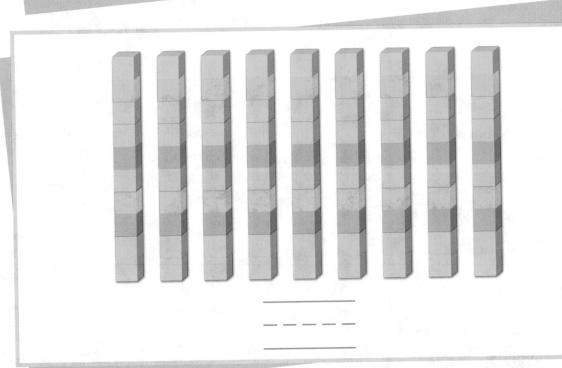

_ _ _ _ _ _

Count Tens

Each stack is made from 10 blocks. Count the stacks. Write a number that ends with 00 to show how many are in the group.

$$\text{-----}$$

Start with 10. Keep counting by tens. Write the missing numbers.

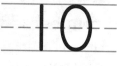 10

100

Color Clues

It is time to find a clue about "Escape from Room Eight"!

"Thanks for showing me your great robot," said Flynn. "Let me make sure I have the facts. The arm might touch Hattie's cage when it moves. It is now two o'clock. The timer made the robot move an hour ago."

"That is all true," said G. Whiz.

"Thanks!" said Flynn. Then, he noticed the position of the robot's arm. What was it? To find out, solve the problems.

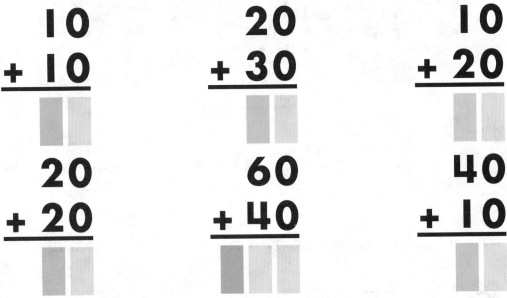

$$10 + 10$$

$$20 + 30$$

$$10 + 20$$

$$20 + 20$$

$$60 + 40$$

$$40 + 10$$

Now, find the numbers you wrote above that match the numbers you collected as evidence on pages 68, 76, 88, and 98. Use their colors and the key below to find letters. Unscramble the letters to finish the sentence and form a clue.

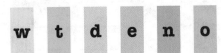

w t d e n o

Clue: What was the position of the robot's arm?

_____ _____ _____

_ _ _ _ _ _ _ _ _ _ _

It was _____ _____ _____.

Write the clue word you found in the Detective's Notebook on pages 202 and 203.

TOP SECRET FILE #3:
Grammar and Vocabulary

Learning Goals:

- Use common nouns, proper nouns, possessive nouns, and pronouns

- Use singular and plural nouns with matching verbs

- Use verbs to describe actions in the present, past, and future

- Use adjectives, conjunctions, prepositions, and articles

- Understand sentences that make statements, give commands, ask questions, and express excitement

- Write dates

- Use commas between words in a series

- Add endings to base words

- Use context clues to find the meaning of words

- Sort words into categories

- Understand that words have different shades of meaning

- Spell words correctly

Collect Evidence on These Evidence Alert! Pages:
Pages 116, 127, 137, 147

Use Evidence to Find a Clue on the Clue Corner Page:
Page 154

Clue Question:
Who did it?

Suspect:
Pete Petty

Common or Proper?

Nouns name people, places, and things. Common nouns such as **boy** and **school** begin with lowercase letters. Proper nouns such as **Pete** and **Sunnyside School** name specific people, places, and things. They always begin with capital letters. Write each noun in the correct column. If it is a proper noun, capitalize it.

mexico   ms. minder

hamster   country

boy   flynn

teacher   hattie

Common Nouns

Proper Nouns

Names Are Nouns

Rewrite the story. Capitalize each proper noun.

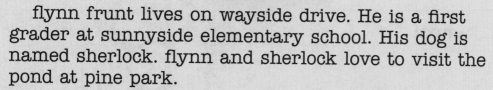

flynn frunt lives on wayside drive. He is a first grader at sunnyside elementary school. His dog is named sherlock. flynn and sherlock love to visit the pond at pine park.

Who Owns It?

To show ownership, add an apostrophe and **s** (**'s**) at the end of a noun. Add **'s** to each noun.

Hattie_____ wheel

the girl_____ backpack

Flynn_____ notebook

the group_____ table

my friend_____ book

Show the Owner

Complete each sentence with a noun that shows who or what owns something. Add **'s** to the noun shown below each blank.

1. The _____ cafeteria is noisy.
   school

2. _____ dad packs his lunch every day.
   Pete

3. The _____ door was open.
   room

4. _____ lunch had a juicy apple.
   Flynn

Noun-Verb Match

When a sentence tells about something that is happening right now, look at the noun in the sentence. If it names one person, place, or thing, the matching verb often ends with **s**. (Example: Flynn **looks** around.) If the noun is plural, the verb often does not end with **s**. (Example: The students **work**.) Circle a verb to complete each sentence. Write it in the blank.

1. The students in room eight _____ lunch

   eats   eat

   before recess.

2. Flynn _____ the class back

   leads   lead

   to room eight at one o'clock.

3. Hattie often _____ on her wheel.

   runs   run

4. G. Whiz, Pete Petty, and Joy Ride _____

   visits   visit

   the science center a lot.

5. Ms. Minder _____ the students with their

   helps   help

   science projects.

It Is Happening Now

When a sentence tells about something that is happening right now, use a present-tense verb. Circle the sentences that tell what is happening now. Underline the verb in each sentence you circle.

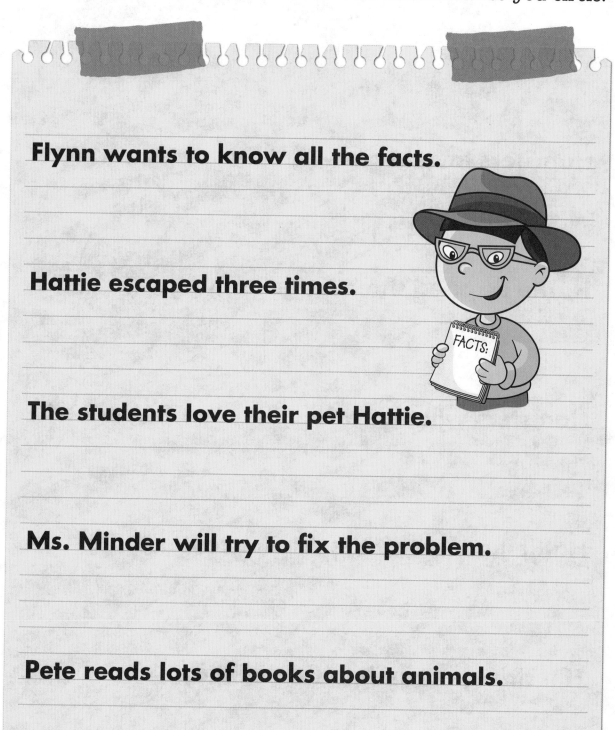

Flynn wants to know all the facts.

Hattie escaped three times.

The students love their pet Hattie.

Ms. Minder will try to fix the problem.

Pete reads lots of books about animals.

It Already Happened

When a sentence tells about something that already happened, use a past-tense verb. Circle the sentences that tell what already happened. Underline the verb in each sentence you circle.

Hamsters love to crawl in tubes.

Hattie escaped three times.

Hamsters will hide when they are frightened.

Hattie jumped off the science center table.

The class pet ran into the hallway.

It Will Happen

When a sentence tells about something that will happen, use a future-tense verb. Circle the sentences that tell what will happen. Underline the verb in each sentence you circle.

Pete filled Hattie's food dish.

The students will try to keep Hattie safe.

Pete will close the cage door tightly.

Pete pets Hattie every day.

Ms. Minder will ask the students to clean up.

Verb Tense Test

It is time to collect more evidence about "Escape from Room Eight."

Pete Petty stood near the cage. "May I ask you some questions?" said Flynn.

"Sure," said Pete. "You want to know about me and Hattie, right?"

"I know you like to take care of her," said Flynn.

"I do! I love animals," explained Pete. "I brush her and pet her. Every week, I bring something from home for her." What does Pete bring? To find out, write a verb in each sentence that matches the tense shown.

Evidence ALERT!

brought	feed	found	will latch

1. The students _____ Hattie's cage tightly from now on.
   Future Tense

2. Flynn _____ Hattie running into the hallway.
   Past Tense

3. Pete _____ something for Hattie last week.
   Past Tense

4. It is a student's job to _____ Hattie every day.
   Present Tense

Find the underlined letters in the verbs you wrote. Write them, in order, in the blanks to make a word that completes the sentence.

Every week, Pete brings Hattie a cardboard _____ _____ _____.

You found evidence! Use the word you wrote to help you find a clue on page 154.

Personal Pronouns

A pronoun takes the place of a noun. Write a pronoun that could take the place of each underlined noun.

she	it	they	he

1. <u>Ms. Minder</u> frowned. _____ was worried about Hattie.

2. First, the <u>students</u> in room eight have lunch. Then, _____ go to recess.

3. <u>Flynn</u> thought for a while. _____ had an idea.

4. There is a <u>robot</u> in the science center. _____ has an arm that goes up and down.

5. <u>Pete and Flynn</u> played at recess. _____ played on the swings.

Possessive Pronouns

Possessive pronouns show ownership. Complete each sentence with a possessive pronoun that matches the underlined pronoun.

her	its	his	my	their

1. <u>It</u> has a plastic floor. _____ walls are metal bars.

2. <u>She</u> rides bus 42. _____ bus arrives at 8:40.

3. <u>They</u> are working on science projects. _____ projects are almost done.

4. <u>He</u> has many questions. Will _____ questions be answered?

5. <u>I</u> am a student in room eight. _____ class has a pet hamster.

Indefinite Pronouns

Some pronouns do not refer to specific people, places, or things.
Choose an indefinite pronoun to complete each sentence.

anyone	everything	everyone	something

1. Does _____ know how Hattie escaped?

2. Please make sure _____ has a seat.

3. Would you like _____ to drink?

4. _____ is ready for the science fair.

A Place for Prepositions

Prepositions show relationships between people, places, and things. Draw a line from each preposition to a phrase where it fits. There is more than one right answer for each preposition.

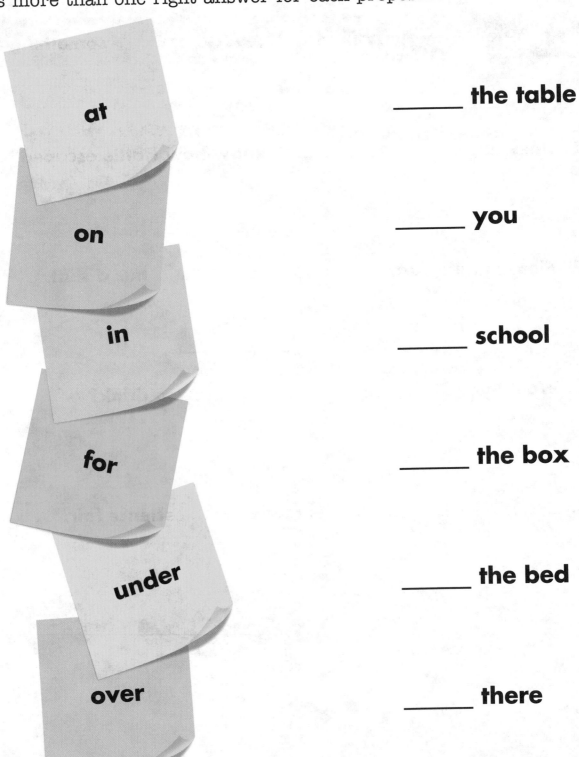

at

on

in

for

under

over

_____ the table

_____ you

_____ school

_____ the box

_____ the bed

_____ there

A Place for Prepositions

Draw a line from each preposition to a phrase where it fits. There is more than one right answer for each preposition.

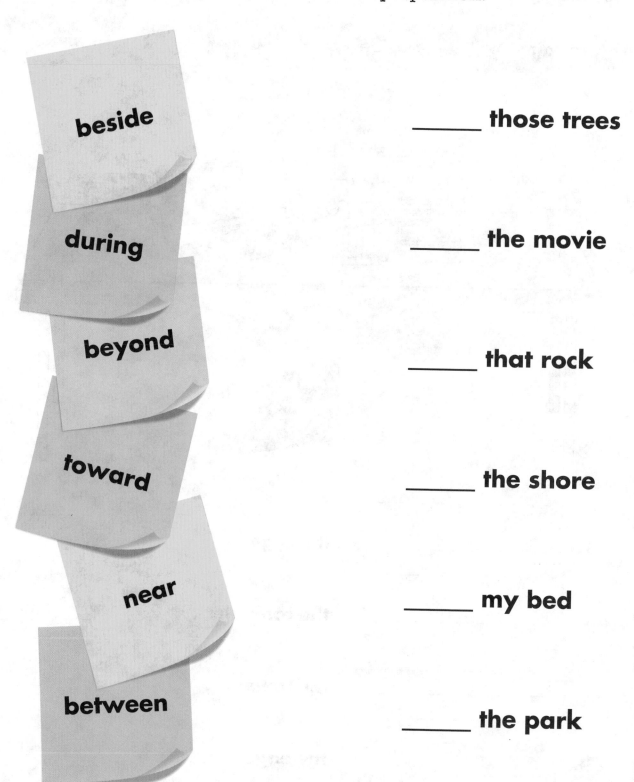

beside

during

beyond

toward

near

between

_____ those trees

_____ the movie

_____ that rock

_____ the shore

_____ my bed

_____ the park

In the Science Center

For each number, write a preposition that describes where something is in the science center.

against	beside	under	near

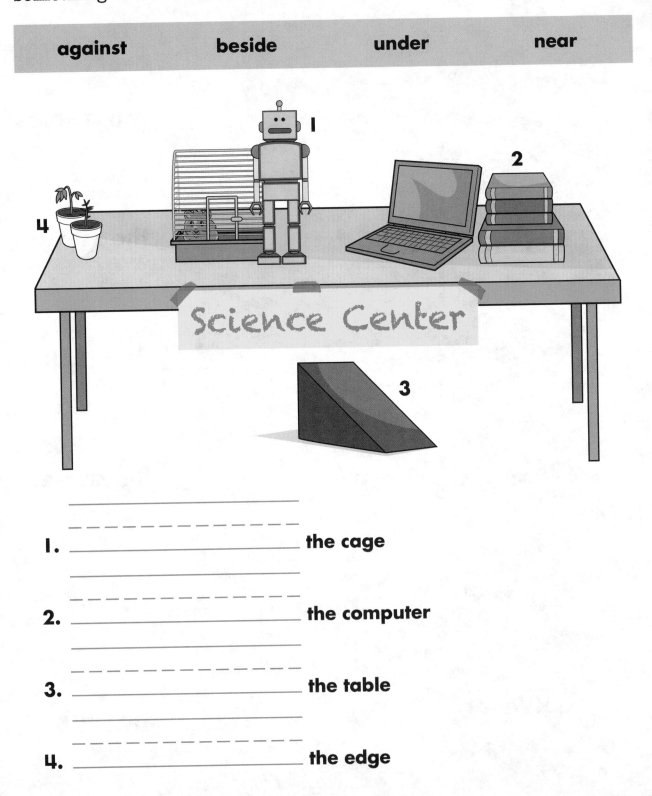

1. _____ the cage

2. _____ the computer

3. _____ the table

4. _____ the edge

Articles

The little words **a** and **an** are articles. They are often used before nouns. Use **a** before words that begin with a consonant sound. Use **an** before words that begin with a vowel sound. Write **a** or **an** in each blank.

_____ **investigator**

_____ **pet**

_____ **table**

_____ **escape**

_____ **idea**

_____ **question**

_____ **notebook**

_____ **hamster**

_____ **apple**

_____ **eye**

Describe It

Adjectives describe nouns. Write a word to describe each noun.

sweet	pesky	hard	sharp	round	purple

_____ **scissors**

_____ **book**

_____ **fly**

_____ **lemonade**

_____ **rock**

_____ **globe**

Describe It

Write an adjective to describe each noun.

| striped | two | furry | happy | spicy | untied |

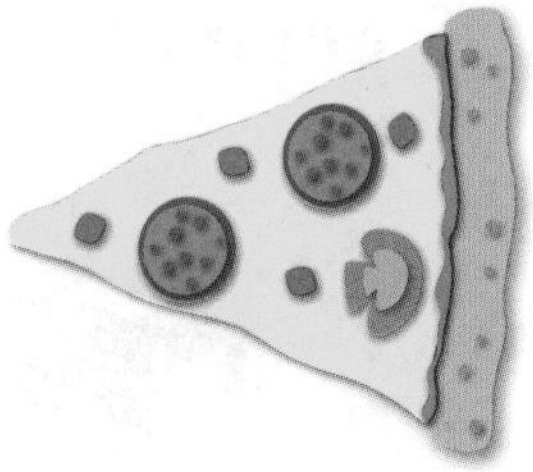

_____
- - - - - - - - -
_____ **pizza**

_____
- - - - - - - - -
_____ **hamster**

_____
- - - - - - - - -
_____ **children**

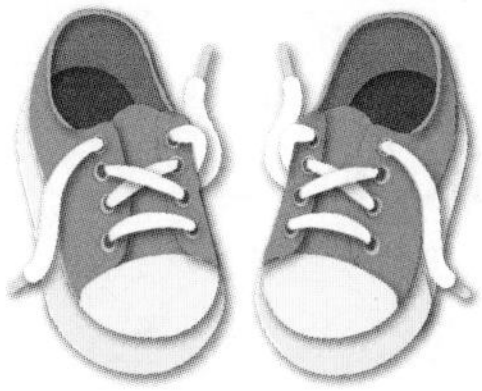

_____
- - - - - - - - -
_____ **shoes**

_____
- - - - - - - - -
_____ **cars**

_____
- - - - - - - - -
_____ **tape**

Adjectives On Your Own

Write your own adjective to complete each sentence.

1. Pete Petty likes _____ animals.

2. He likes _____ dogs.

3. He likes _____ cats.

4. He likes _____ birds.

5. He even likes _____ hamsters!

Name

Key Words

Evidence ALERT!

It is time to collect more evidence about "Escape from Room Eight."

"I study animals and learn how to take care of them," Pete continued. "I check to make sure Hattie's eyes are bright and shiny. I brush her fur so it is smooth and clean. I even check these every day to make sure they have no cuts or splinters." What does Pete check every day? To find out, choose words to write in each blank.

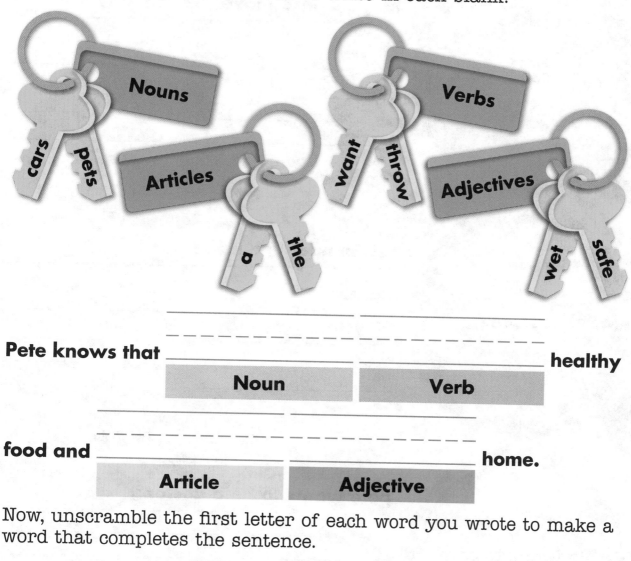

Pete knows that _____ _____ **healthy**

| Noun | Verb |

_____

food and _____ _____ **home.**

| Article | Adjective |

Now, unscramble the first letter of each word you wrote to make a word that completes the sentence.

_____ _____ _____ _____

Pete checks Hattie's _____ _____ _____ _____ **every day.**

You found evidence! Use the word you wrote to help you find a clue on page 154.

Telling Sentences

Some sentences provide information, or tell something. They begin with a capital letter. They end with a period. Rewrite each sentence correctly. Use the information in the magnifying glass to add an adjective to your sentence.

Her nose is **pink**.

hattie's nose moves up and down

_____

- -

_____

_____

She is **friendly**.

ms. minder is our teacher

_____

- -

_____

_____

He wants to care for **animals**.

pete wants to be a doctor

_____

- -

_____

_____

Commanding Sentences

Some sentences give commands. They begin with a capital letter. They end with a period. Rewrite each sentence correctly. Use the information in the magnifying glass to add an adjective to your sentence.

close the door

The door goes to the **classroom**.

try to find information

Information is **useful**.

water the plants

The plants are **new**.

Sentences That Ask Questions

Some sentences ask questions. They begin with a capital letter. They end with a question mark. Use the words around each wheel to write a question correctly.

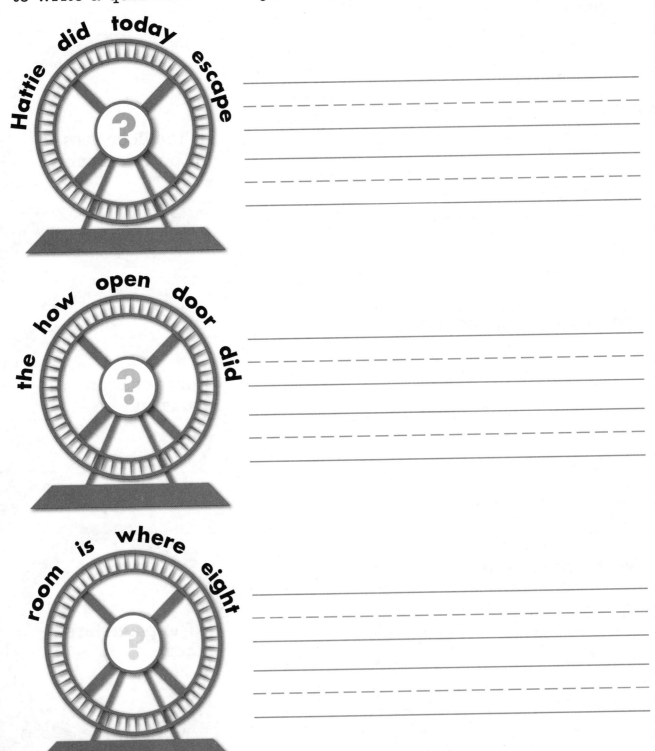

did today
Hattie escape

_____
- - - - - - - - - - - - - - - - - - -
_____
- - - - - - - - - - - - - - - - - - -
_____

open
how door
the did

_____
- - - - - - - - - - - - - - - - - - -
_____
- - - - - - - - - - - - - - - - - - -
_____

is where
room eight

_____
- - - - - - - - - - - - - - - - - - -
_____
- - - - - - - - - - - - - - - - - - -
_____

Name

Sentences That Show Excitement

Some sentences show excitement. They begin with a capital letter. They end with an exclamation mark. Use the words around each wheel to write an exclamation correctly.

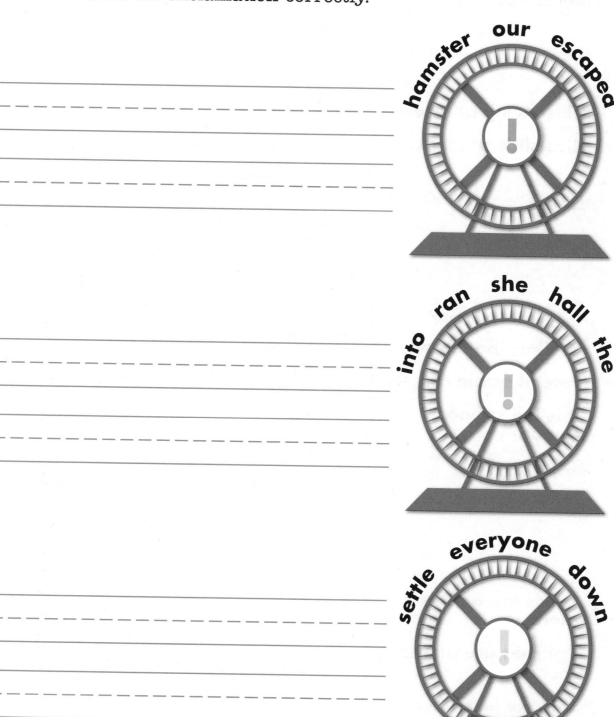

Simple Sentences

Read the sentences. Then, write one sentence that gives all the information. You will need to add the joining word **and** to each sentence you write.

Kids swing at recess.

Kids slide at recess.

G. likes the center.

Pete likes the center.

It is the science center.

Tacos are on the menu.

Peaches are on the menu.

It is the lunch menu.

Compound Sentences

In a compound sentence, two simple sentences are joined together with a joining word. Read the first two compound sentences. Then, use crayons to color the words in the last sentence to match.

Flynn asked questions, and Pete answered.

Joining Word

Pets are fun, but they need lots of care.

Joining Word

I can choose the writing center, or I can choose the science center.

Joining Word

Get It Together

Read the sentences. Then, write one simple or compound sentence that gives all the information. Use the joining word shown. Do not forget to add capital letters and end marks.

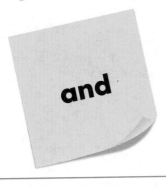

and

does flynn lead the line to lunch

does flynn lead the line to recess

_____

- - - - - - - - - - - - - - - - - - - -

_____

- - - - - - - - - - - - - - - - - - - -

_____

so

pete finished his work

he can go to the science center

_____

- - - - - - - - - - - - - - - - - - - -

_____

- - - - - - - - - - - - - - - - - - - -

_____

- - - - - - - - - - - - - - - - - - - -

_____

Get It Together

Read the sentences. Then, write one simple or compound sentence that gives all the information. Use the joining word shown. Do not forget to add capital letters and end marks.

did hattie escape

the cage door was open

pete tried to watch birds

it was too dark outside

Words That Join

Joining words include **and**, **but**, **or**, **so**, and **yet**. Circle one or more joining words in each sentence.

Pete Petty is seven years old, and he goes to Sunnyside School.

At recess, Pete likes to climb and swing, or he likes to play foursquare.

Pete loves animals, so he has lots of books about them.

Pete often jokes around, yet he is a good student.

Pete likes mammals and reptiles, but he likes insects and birds, too.

Color Code

Evidence ALERT!

It is time to collect more evidence about "Escape from Room Eight."

"Hattie helps me do science experiments," said Pete. "I collect data about how much she eats each day. I want to find out if she eats more on days when students are at school than she does on weekends. I also take notes about how much time she spends doing this." What does Pete take notes about? To find out, write a joining word (**and, but, so**) to complete each sentence.

A hamster is smaller than a guinea pig, _____

it is larger than a mouse.

Joy's name is on the job chart, _____ **it is her**

turn to feed Hattie.

Do not feed a hamster peanut butter _____

jelly.

Now, find one letter that is shared by all the words with the same color. Write the letters to find a word that completes the sentence.

Pete takes notes about how long Hattie ▢▢▢▢ on her wheel.

You found evidence! Use the word you wrote to help you find a clue on page 154.

Add an Ending

Add endings to the verbs. Complete the chart. You may need to change the spelling of the base word before the ending is added. The first row is done for you.

	–s	–ed	–ing
work	works	worked	working
share			
pet			
carry			
stop			

Name

Paw Print Pairs

Choose a base word. Combine it with a prefix or a suffix from the paw prints to make a new word. You may need to change the spelling of the base word. Write the new words on the lines.

play	lock	do	take
match	lead	help	watch

mis-   -er   re-

-ful   -ed   un-

Words That Are Alike

In each row, circle the word whose meaning is most like the meaning of the first word.

grin	frown	smile	mouth
bag	grocery	backpack	sack
little	tiny	huge	size
nice	angry	friend	kind
tired	nap	sleepy	awake
shout	whisper	talk	yell

Words That Are Different

In each row, circle the word whose meaning is unlike the meaning of the first word.

hot   warm   freezing   cozy

fast   poky   swift   quick

happy   glad   feeling   glum

sick   achy   hurt   healthy

quiet   hushed   talking   noisy

graceful   clumsy   dancer   clown

Cross One Out

Cross out one word in each group that does not belong.

paper
pencils
quarters
books

lake
hill
ocean
pond

park
library
store
airplane

ribbon
tulip
rose
daisy

cat
otter
snake
raccoon

bowl
pot
blanket
spoon

boy
sand
shell
crab

gloves
shorts
coat
scarf

love
idea
hope
fear

Choose a Center

Write each word in the center where it belongs.

paints seeds	dictionary dice	token glitter	hamster envelope

Art Center

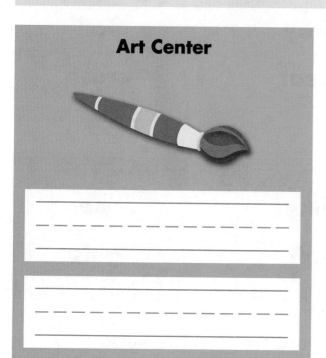

_____

_____

Science Center

_____

_____

Writing Center

_____

_____

Game Center

_____

_____

Many Meanings

In each pair of words, circle the word that has the stronger meaning.

scream say	okay great	fall crash
close slam	silky soft	sip gulp

In each pair of words, circle the word that has the weaker meaning.

nervous terrified	exhausted sleepy	boiling hot
small tiny	sprint jog	ask beg

Spell and Write

Circle the correctly spelled word to finish each sentence. Write it in the blank.

1. Please give this note _____ Flynn.

   two   toe   to

2. Are _____ in room eight?

   you   yoo   ewe

3. Ms. Minder _____ worried.

   was   wuz   waz

4. These supplies are _____ the science

   form   from   frum

   center.

5. _____ is Pete's experiment.

   Theer   Their   There

6. Write the answer on the _____ .

   boord   board   bord

Spell and Write

Circle the correctly spelled word to finish each sentence. Write it in the blank.

1. Do you _____ to see Hattie?

   | went | want | wunt |

2. Ms. Minder helps us _____.

   | learn | lern | lurn |

3. Can the robot _____ its arm?

   | move | moov | muve |

4. It is time to _____ to the cafeteria.

   | wok | walk | wock |

5. The students _____ reading.

   | where | were | wir |

Follow the Path

It is time to collect more evidence about "Escape from Room Eight."

"Do you ever take Hattie out of her cage?" Flynn asked Pete.

"Well..." Pete began. "I have taken her out the past few days. But only for an important experiment! I built something special for her to run through. I use a timer to see how fast she goes." What did Pete build? To find out, draw a path through the letters needed to spell a word that completes the sentence.

It is not safe for Hattie to be _____ of her cage.

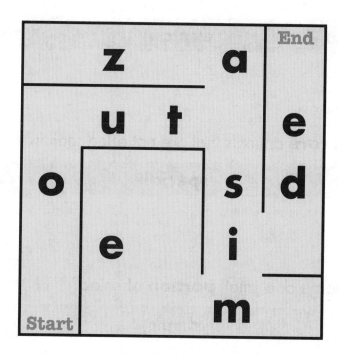

Four letters in the puzzle were not used. Unscramble them to make a word that completes the sentence.

Pete made a ____ ____ ____ ____ for Hattie to run through.

You found evidence! Use the word you wrote to help you find a clue on page 154.

It Makes Sense!

Use the sentence to decide the meaning of each **bold** word. Circle your choice.

The blue paint turned a **pale** color when we added water to it.

dark	bucket	light

Ms. Minder asked us to listen the first time so she does not have to **repeat** herself.

think about	explain	say again

Pete is interested in **rare** animals that are not often seen in the wild.

scary	special	common

Would you like a large or a small **portion** of salad?

amount	drink	bowl

Wear a hat to **shield** you from the bright sunlight.

collect	protect	burn

Name

It Makes Sense!

Use the sentence to decide the meaning of each **bold** word. Circle your choice.

The day was sunny, warm, and **pleasant**.

dull	sad	nice

Most of the students were reading, but some **individuals** chose to do puzzles instead.

people	adults	things

We used an air tank to **inflate** the balloons.

break	fill with air	make

When Hattie escaped, room eight was loud and **hectic**.

crazy	calm	scary

Try to stand still so you do not **jostle** the person next to you in line.

bother	talk to	bump

Commas in Between

When you write a list of things in a sentence, put a comma after each item. Write commas where they belong. The first one is done for you.

1. Pete carried his backpack, lunch box, and jacket.

2. Hattie needs food water and clean bedding.

3. Flynn has questions for G. Whiz Pete and Joy.

4. Ms. Minder asked us to choose a game choose a partner and play quietly.

5. For this project, you will need paper scissors glue and a paper bag.

Commas in Between

Write commas where they belong.

1. Hattie likes to crawl in tunnels run on her wheel and take naps.

2. Students in room eight like art class gym class and music class.

3. The science center has plants rocks and feathers.

4. Hattie escaped from her cage on Monday Tuesday and Wednesday.

5. Pete's favorite insects are bees ladybugs ants and butterflies.

Great Dates

When you write a date, capitalize the name of the month. Write a comma between the number that tells the day and the number that tells the year. Look at important dates from Pete's life. Write each one correctly on the line.

Pete was born.

june 12 2009

_____

Pete's family moved to a new town.

october 22 2010

_____

Pete got a puppy.

december 25 2012

_____

Great Dates

Look at important dates from Pete's life. Write each one correctly on the line.

Pete got a kitten.

march 17 2013

_____

- - - - - - - - - - - - - - - - - -

_____

Pete started kindergarten.

august 28 2015

_____

- - - - - - - - - - - - - - - - - -

_____

Pete turned seven years old.

june 12 2016

_____

- - - - - - - - - - - - - - - - - -

_____

CLUE CORNER

Take Note!

It is time to find a clue about "Escape from Room Eight"!

"After your experiments, do you always put Hattie back in her cage and latch the door?" asked Flynn.

"I think so," said Pete. "I am pretty sure I do. Anyway, I did not think Hattie could get down from the table by herself. I never taught her to..." What did Pete think that Hattie could not do? To find out, write the words you collected as evidence on pages 116, 127, 137, and 147 to complete the sentences. Add the missing commas and end punctuation marks.

Hattie has a food dish a water bottle and
—— —— —— ——

a cardboard —— —— ——
＊

Does Pete watch when Hattie eats goes through the
—— —— —— —— —— —— —— ——

—— —— —— —— —— —— —— ——

—— —— —— —— **and** —— —— —— —— **on her wheel**
☺ ✕

On October 10 2016, Pete found splinters in Hattie's
—— —— —— ——

—— —— —— ——
☆

Now, use the letters above the symbols to write a word that completes the sentence.

Clue: Why did Pete think Hattie was safe?

—— —— —— ——

Pete did not think Hattie could —— —— —— —— .
✕ ＊ ☺ ☆

Write the clue word you found in the Detective's Notebook on pages 202 and 203.

TOP SECRET FILE #4:
Two-Digit Numbers, Measurement, and Shapes

Learning Goals:

- Add and subtract multiples of 10
- Understand and compare two-digit numbers
- Add two-digit numbers within 100
- Measure length in units
- Tell time to the half-hour
- Understand important characteristics of shapes
- Use shapes in drawing
- Divide shapes into halves and quarters

Collect Evidence on These Evidence Alert! Pages:
Pages 165, 175, 187, 198

Use Evidence to Find a Clue on the Clue Corner Page:
Page 201

Clue Question:
Who did it?

Suspect:
Joy Ride

Take Away Tens

Cross out tens blocks to help you solve the subtraction problems.

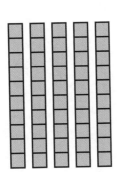

50 – 10 = _____

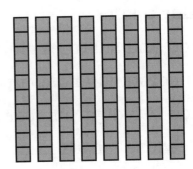

80 – 30 = _____

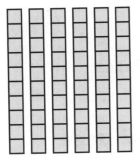

60 – 60 = _____

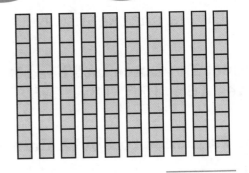

100 – 30 = _____

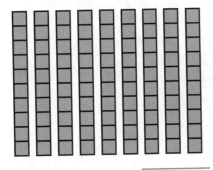

90 – 50 = _____

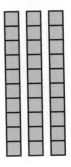

30 – 10 = _____

Name

Thinking in Tens

Solve each equation. Then, circle **True** or **False**.

$10 + 40 = $ _____

$30 + 30 = $ _____

$60 + 20 = $ _____

$50 + 30 = $ _____

$10 + 40 = 30 + 30$

True

False

$60 + 20 = 50 + 30$

True

False

$90 - 70 = $ _____

$80 - 50 = $ _____

$40 - 20 = $ _____

$70 - 50 = $ _____

$90 - 70 = 80 - 50$

True

False

$40 - 20 = 70 - 50$

True

False

Plus and Minus 10

Look at the number on each car. Write the number that is 10 less. Write the number that is 10 more.

−10   40   +10

−10   16   +10

−10   58   +10

Plus and Minus 10

Look at the number on each car. Write the number that is 10 less.
Write the number that is 10 more.

−10   37   +10

−10   88   +10

−10   21   +10

Pinball Place Value

Write numbers to complete the chart. The first one is done for you.

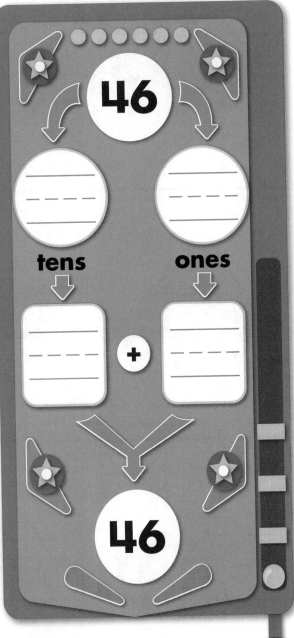

Pinball Place Value

Write numbers to complete the charts.

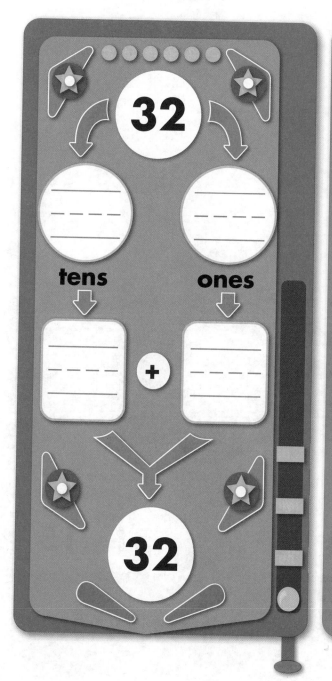

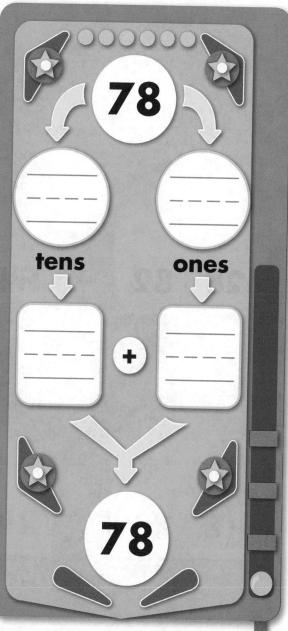

Which Door Is More?

On each house, draw a door around the number that is greater.

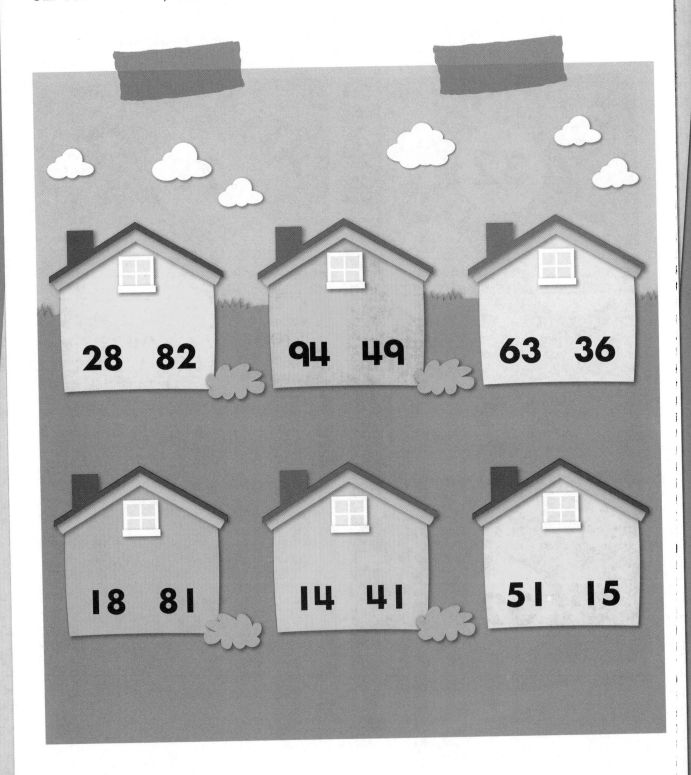

28   82

94   49

63   36

18   81

14   41

51   15

Which Door Is Less?

On each house, draw a door around the number that is less.

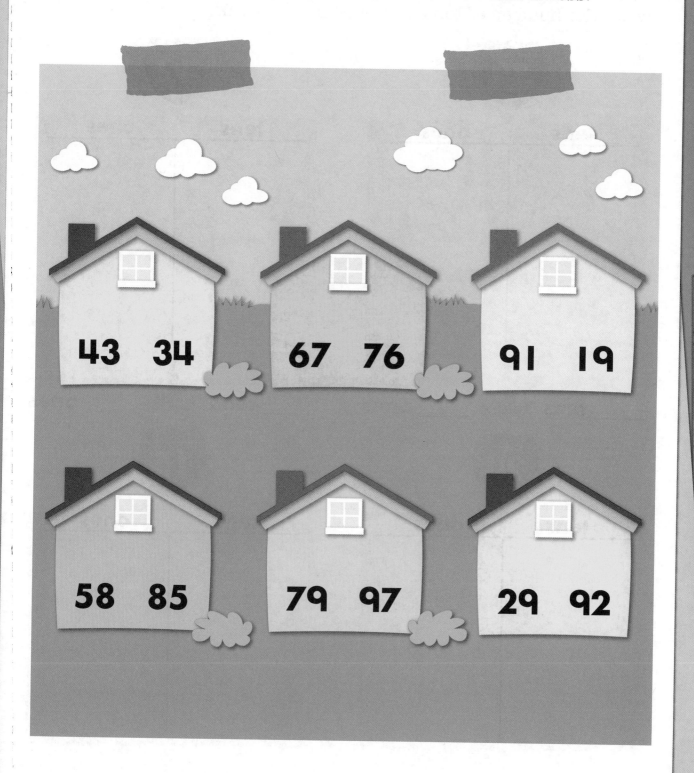

43 34

67 76

91 19

58 85

79 97

29 92

Road Rules

Draw tens blocks and ones blocks to show each number. Then, write the number of tens and ones in the blanks.

39

tens	ones

_____ tens _____ ones

42

tens	ones

_____ tens _____ ones

24

tens	ones

_____ tens _____ ones

15

tens	ones

_____ ten _____ ones

Name

Middle of the Road

It is time to collect more evidence about "Escape from Room Eight."

Flynn Frunt had one more student to talk to. He found Joy Ride drawing a picture. "What a cool race car!" Flynn said.

"Thanks!" said Joy. "I bet this car would go fast. I tested one like it on my ramp."

"In the science center?" asked Flynn.

"Yes, I am testing a new kind of toy vehicle each week to see how fast it goes," explained Joy. "Guess how many vehicles have gone down the ramp so far." How many vehicles has Joy tested? To find out, write the numbers on the road in order from least to greatest.

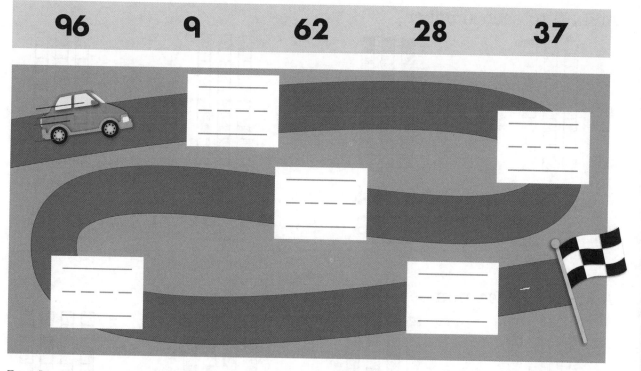

Look at the numbers you wrote. Which one is in the middle space on the road? Write it to complete the sentence.

_____

_ _ _ _ _

Joy has tested _____ vehicles.

You found evidence! Use the number you wrote to help you find a clue on page 201.

Add Some Tens

Add 20 to each number.

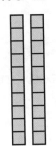 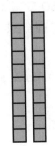 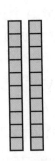 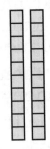

$$\begin{array}{r} 56 \\ +\ 20 \\ \hline \end{array}$$
$$\begin{array}{r} 8 \\ +\ 20 \\ \hline \end{array}$$
$$\begin{array}{r} 42 \\ +\ 20 \\ \hline \end{array}$$
$$\begin{array}{r} 71 \\ +\ 20 \\ \hline \end{array}$$

Add 30 to each number.

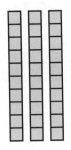 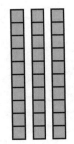 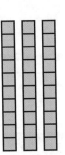 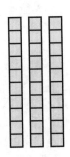

$$\begin{array}{r} 11 \\ +\ 30 \\ \hline \end{array}$$
$$\begin{array}{r} 44 \\ +\ 30 \\ \hline \end{array}$$
$$\begin{array}{r} 67 \\ +\ 30 \\ \hline \end{array}$$
$$\begin{array}{r} 21 \\ +\ 30 \\ \hline \end{array}$$

Add 40 to each number.

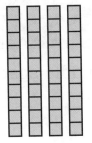 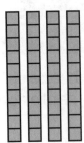 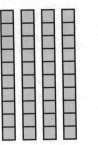 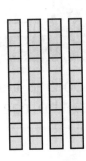

$$\begin{array}{r} 56 \\ +\ 40 \\ \hline \end{array}$$
$$\begin{array}{r} 12 \\ +\ 40 \\ \hline \end{array}$$
$$\begin{array}{r} 39 \\ +\ 40 \\ \hline \end{array}$$
$$\begin{array}{r} 6 \\ +\ 40 \\ \hline \end{array}$$

Name

Add Some Tens

Add 50 to each number.

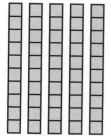
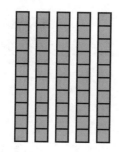
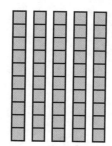
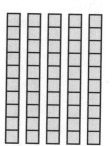

38	0	41	19
+ 50	+ 50	+ 50	+ 50

Add 60 to each number.

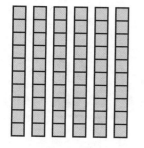
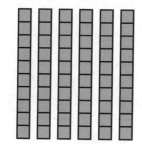
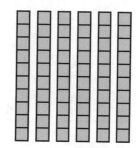
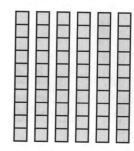

2	33	25	16
+ 60	+ 60	+ 60	+ 60

Add 70 to each number.

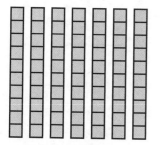
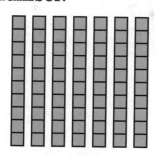
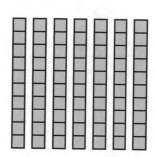
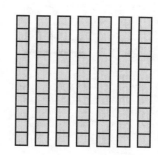

23	14	5	19
+ 70	+ 70	+ 70	+ 70

Ones, Then Tens

To solve each problem, add the ones first. Then, add the tens.

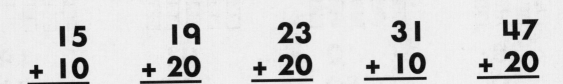

15 + 10	19 + 20	23 + 20	31 + 10	47 + 20

13 + 30	29 + 40	17 + 40	11 + 50	60 + 30

75 + 10	50 + 40	25 + 70	42 + 50	12 + 80

Ones, Then Tens

To solve each problem, add the ones first. Then, add the tens.

$$
\begin{array}{r} 18 \\ + 20 \\ \hline \end{array}
\qquad
\begin{array}{r} 13 \\ + 70 \\ \hline \end{array}
\qquad
\begin{array}{r} 20 \\ + 40 \\ \hline \end{array}
\qquad
\begin{array}{r} 59 \\ + 20 \\ \hline \end{array}
\qquad
\begin{array}{r} 15 \\ + 70 \\ \hline \end{array}
$$

$$
\begin{array}{r} 17 \\ + 40 \\ \hline \end{array}
\qquad
\begin{array}{r} 11 \\ + 20 \\ \hline \end{array}
\qquad
\begin{array}{r} 49 \\ + 30 \\ \hline \end{array}
\qquad
\begin{array}{r} 86 \\ + 10 \\ \hline \end{array}
\qquad
\begin{array}{r} 25 \\ + 50 \\ \hline \end{array}
$$

Two Digits Plus One

Add the purple blocks to the blue blocks. Write the sums.

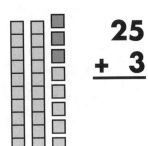
$$25 + 3$$

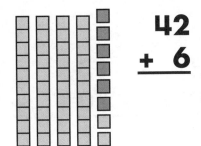
$$42 + 6$$

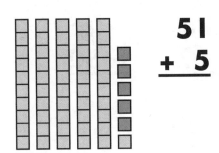
$$51 + 5$$

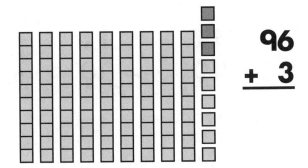
$$96 + 3$$

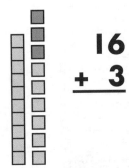
$$16 + 3$$

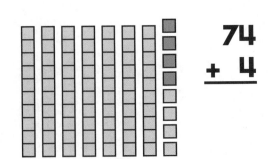
$$74 + 4$$

Name

Add Some Ones

Write 0 in each empty box. Then, find the sums. Add the ones.
Then, add the tens.

```
  15        20        13        22
+ ☐2      + ☐6      + ☐4      + ☐6
_____    _____    _____    _____


  47        14        63        53
+ ☐2      + ☐1      + ☐5      + ☐6
_____    _____    _____    _____


  87        41        34        71
+ ☐2      + ☐4      + ☐5      + ☐7
_____    _____    _____    _____
```

Regroup a Ten

Add the purple blocks to the blue blocks. Notice that the sum of the ones blocks is more than 10. Regroup by adding 1 ten to the tens column in each problem. The first one is done for you.

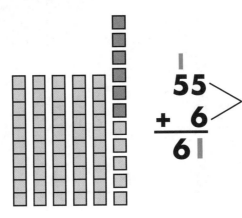

$$\begin{array}{r} 1 \\ 55 \\ + 6 \\ \hline 61 \end{array}$$

$$\begin{array}{r} 5 \\ + 6 \\ \hline 11 \end{array}$$

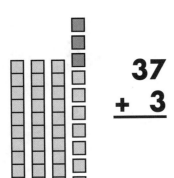

$$\begin{array}{r} 37 \\ + 3 \\ \hline \end{array}$$

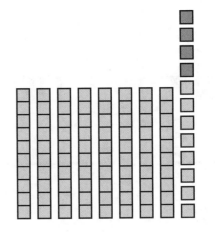

$$\begin{array}{r} 88 \\ + 4 \\ \hline \end{array}$$

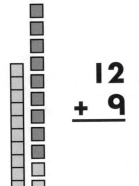

$$\begin{array}{r} 12 \\ + 9 \\ \hline \end{array}$$

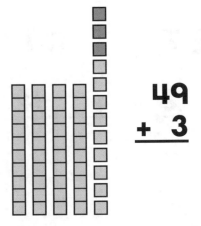

$$\begin{array}{r} 49 \\ + 3 \\ \hline \end{array}$$

Regroup a Ten

Add the purple blocks to the blue blocks. Notice that the sum of the ones blocks is more than 10. Regroup by adding 1 ten to the tens column in each problem.

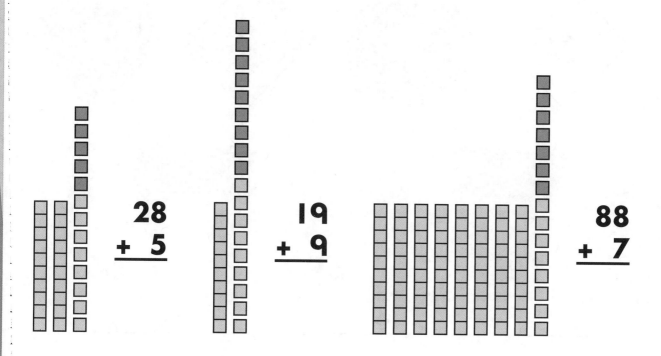

$$28 + 5$$

$$19 + 9$$

$$88 + 7$$

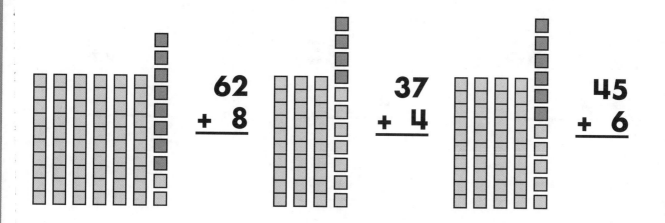

$$62 + 8$$

$$37 + 4$$

$$45 + 6$$

Which Way?

Write numbers from the signs in the boxes to finish the problems.
Solve the problems.

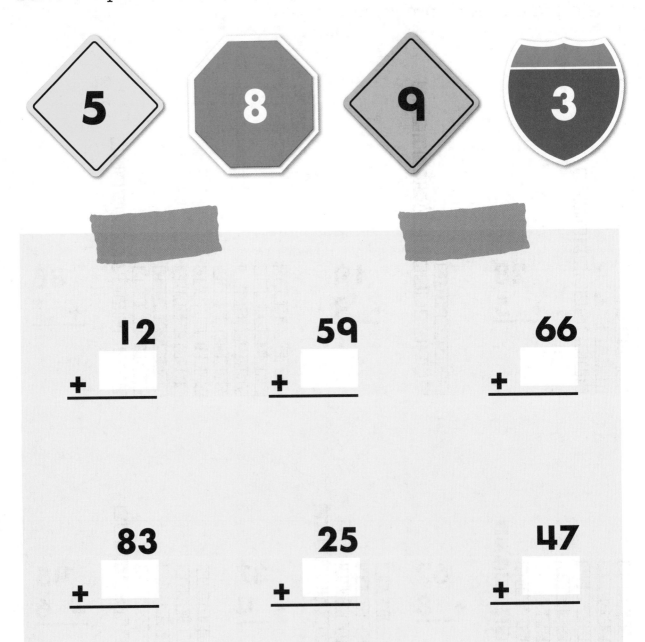

5   8   9   3

12
+ ☐

59
+ ☐

66
+ ☐

83
+ ☐

25
+ ☐

47
+ ☐

Wagon Ride

It is time to collect more evidence about "Escape from Room Eight."

"Let me show you my experiment," offered Joy as she went to the science center.

"Your ramp is in front of Hattie's cage," Flynn noticed.

"I had to move it because G.'s robot and Pete's maze were taking all the space!" complained Joy. "Last week, I tested vehicles with four wheels, like cars and wagons. They start from the top of the ramp. Can you guess how tall it is?" How tall was Joy's ramp? To find out, solve the problems. Write the sums in the wagons.

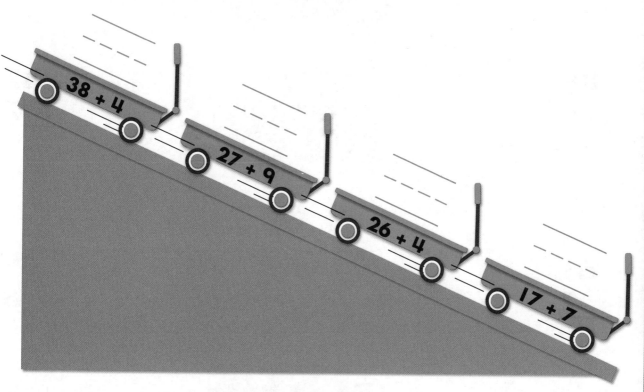

Look at the sums you wrote. They form a pattern going from the top of the ramp to the bottom. What number is next in the pattern? Write it to finish the sentence.

_____

_ _ _ _

Joy Ride's ramp was _____ inches tall.

You found evidence! Use the number you wrote to help you find a clue on page 201.

Make a Match

Solve each problem. Draw a line to the vehicle that shows the sum.

86
+ 6

59
+ 9

92

45
+ 9

47
+ 7

47

61
+ 7

39
+ 8

68

54

42
+ 5

89
+ 3

Make a Match

Solve each problem. Draw a line to the vehicle that shows the sum.

71
+ 4

76
+ 6

26

27
+ 7

17
+ 9

75

20
+ 6

82

29
+ 5

34

78
+ 4

69
+ 6

The Secret Number Is...

Solve the problems in each row. The number that all the sums share is the secret number. Write it in the blank.

The number in the tens place is _____ .

$$49 + 3$$ $$51 + 4$$ $$45 + 5$$

The number in the ones place is _____ .

$$26 + 7$$ $$85 + 8$$ $$69 + 4$$

The number in the tens place is _____ .

$$87 + 3$$ $$93 + 6$$ $$85 + 7$$

The Secret Number Is...

Solve the problems in each row. The number that all the sums share is the secret number. Write it in the blank.

18 + 9	43 + 4	69 + 8

The number in the ones place

is _____ .

36 + 5	44 + 4	33 + 7

The number in the tens place

is _____ .

66 + 6	79 + 3	15 + 7

The number in the ones place

is _____ .

What's the Problem?

Add or subtract.

80 − 50	31 + 20	45 + 6	90 − 30
73 + 10	89 + 4	60 + 25	70 − 40
14 + 80	60 − 10	67 + 9	46 + 3

What's the Problem?

Add or subtract.

$$58 + 7$$

$$20 - 20$$

$$46 + 8$$

$$59 + 20$$

$$90 - 40$$

$$37 + 7$$

$$11 + 50$$

$$29 + 5$$

$$50 - 10$$

$$78 + 6$$

A Long Run

In gym class, the kids in room eight ran on a track. Line up pennies on each track to see the length of each student's run. Then, write the number of pennies that shows the length.

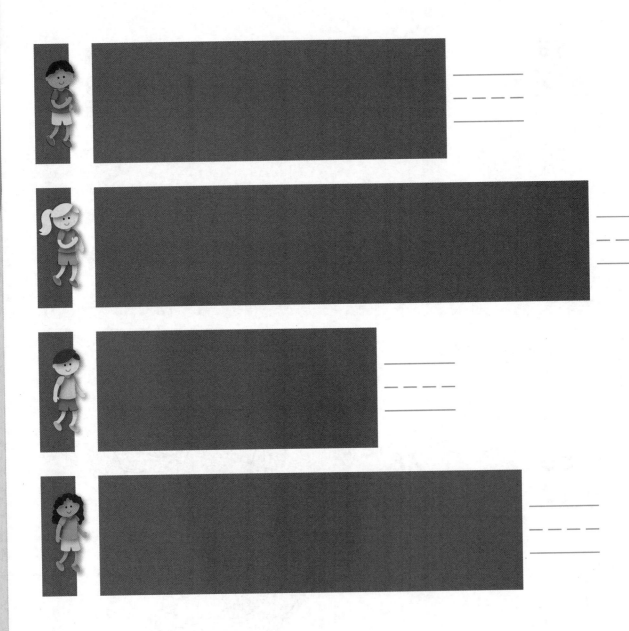

A Long Run

Line up pennies on each track to see the length of each student's run. Then, write the number of pennies that shows the length.

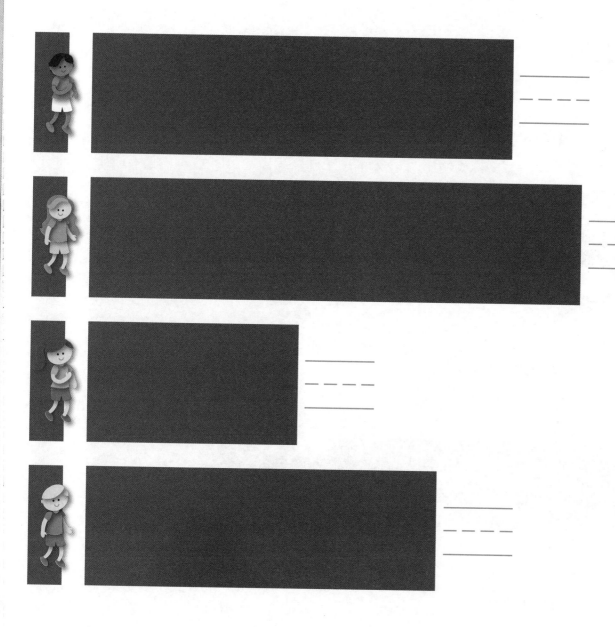

Every Penny Counts

Measure each object with pennies. Lay the pennies end-to-end. Do not leave any gaps. Do not overlap the pennies. Write the measurement on the line.

_____ **penny**

_____ **pennies**

_____ **pennies**

Every Penny Counts

Measure each object with pennies. Lay the pennies end-to-end. Do not leave any gaps. Do not overlap the pennies. Write the measurement on the line.

_____

‒ ‒ ‒

_____ **pennies**

_____

‒ ‒ ‒

_____ **pennies**

_____

‒ ‒ ‒

_____ **pennies**

Thumb-Tastic!

Use the width of your thumb to measure each ribbon. Do not leave any gaps. Do not overlap the thumb-widths. Write the measurement on the line.

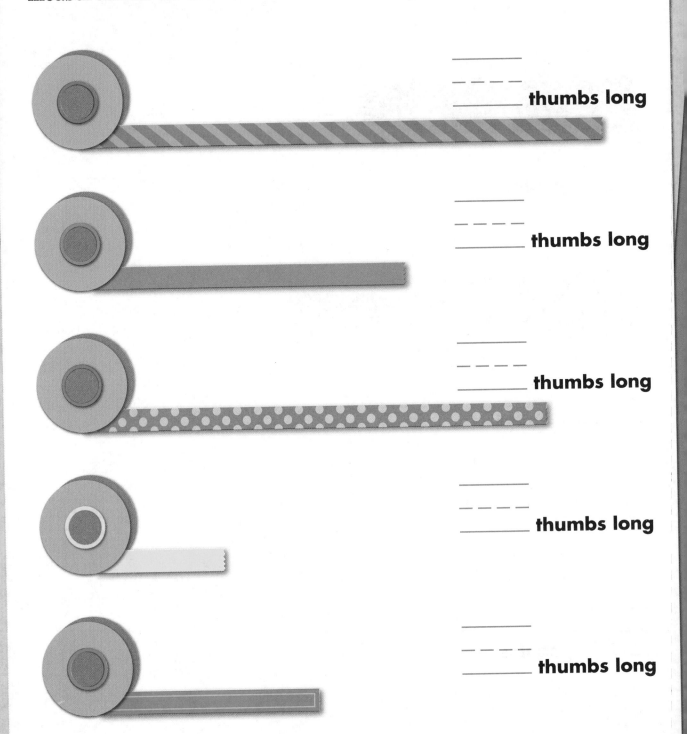

_____ **thumbs long**

_____ **thumbs long**

_____ **thumbs long**

_____ **thumbs long**

_____ **thumbs long**

Bike Path

It is time to collect more evidence about "Escape from Room Eight."

"This week I am testing how fast two-wheeled vehicles like this can go down the ramp," said Joy as she held up a tiny toy bike. "I use a stopwatch to time the bike as it goes down the ramp. Then, I use a penny to measure how far the bike goes on the table after it leaves the ramp. Can you guess how long this bike traveled on the table during my last test?" How far did Joy's toy bike go? To find out, use a penny to measure the path.

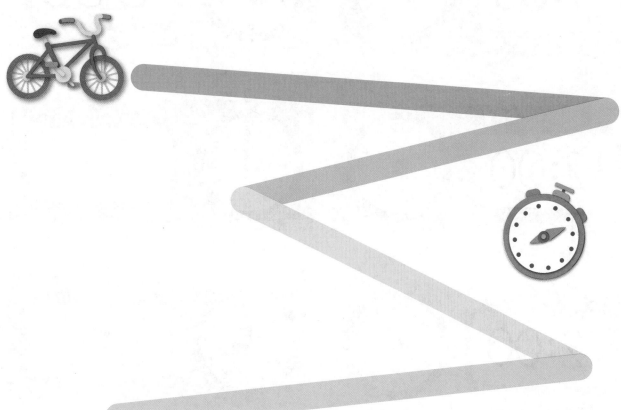

How many pennies long was the path? Write the number to complete the sentence.

_____

_ _ _ _

Joy's toy bike traveled a length of _____ pennies.

You found evidence! Use the number you wrote to help you find a clue on page 201.

Tell the Time: Hours

When the long hand is on 12, the short hand shows the hour.
Draw the missing clock hands or write the missing numbers to
show the time for each clock. The first two are done for you.

 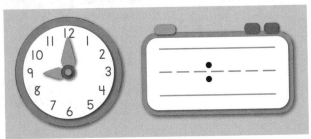

 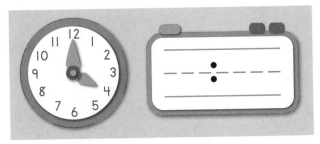

 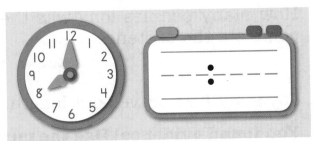

Show the Time: Hours

Draw the missing clock hands and write the missing numbers to show each time.

five o'clock

nine o'clock

one o'clock

Tell the Time: Half-Hours

When the long hand is on 6, the short hand shows the half-hour. Draw the missing clock hands or write the missing numbers to show the time for each clock. The first two are done for you.

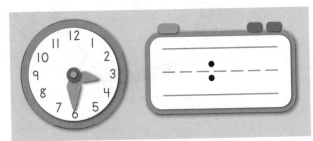

Name

Show the Time: Half-Hours

Draw the missing clock hands and write the missing numbers to show each time.

one thirty

eight thirty

twelve thirty

Two Kinds of Clocks

Draw lines to match the times on two different kinds of clocks.

1:00

8:30

10:00

4:00

1:30

Two Kinds of Clocks

Draw lines to match the times on two different kinds of clocks.

5:00

3:30

11:00

6:30

12:30

Name

Sort the Shapes

Follow the directions.

1. Color each circle.

2. Outline each shape that has 4 sides.

3. Draw an X on each square.

4. Draw a dot in each shape with 3 sides.

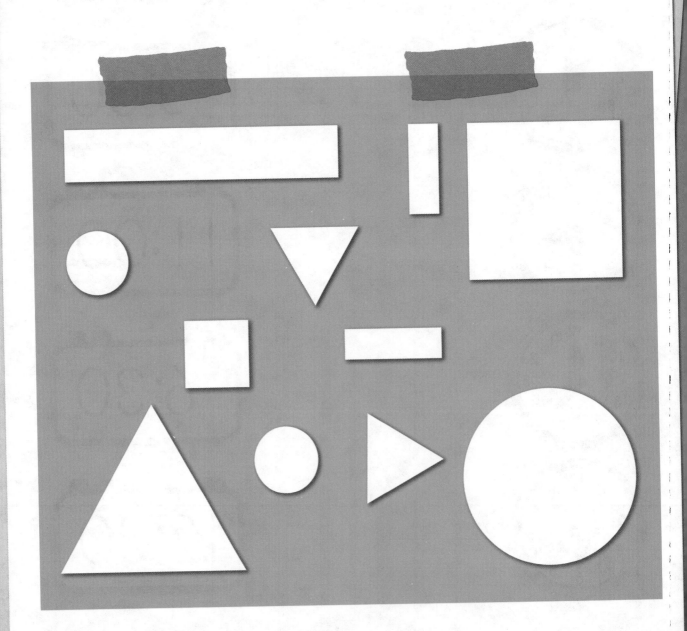

Something in Common

Look at each shape. Does it have straight sides? Curves? Angles? In each box, draw new shapes that have something in common with the shape shown.

Shape Creations

Circle the shapes needed to make each picture.

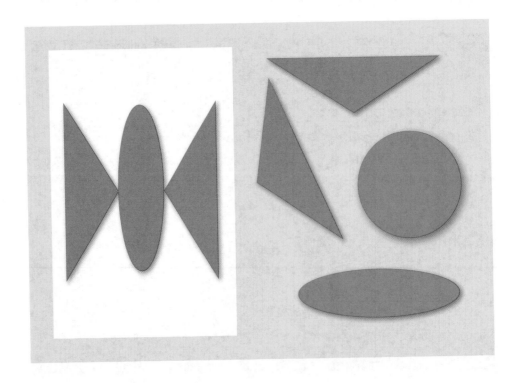

Shape Creations

Circle the shapes needed to make each picture.

Motor Maze

It is time to collect more evidence about
"Escape from Room Eight."

"Are you using more two-wheeled vehicles?"
asked Flynn.

"Yes! Today before lunch I tested this," Joy
explained as she pointed to a little motorcycle. "See, it has two
wheels and handlebars, just like the bike."

"Before lunch? Is that when you do your experiment?" asked
Flynn.

"Yes, every day before lunch," said Joy. "Can you guess how
many seconds in all it took the motorcycle to go down the ramp 10
times?" How many seconds did it take? To find out, color all the
shapes with four sides to make a path for the motorcycle.

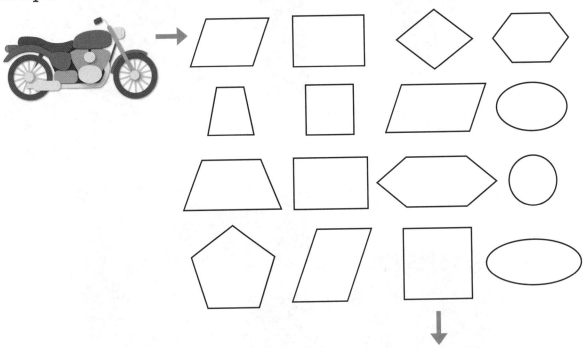

What is the total number of sides for all the shapes you colored?
Write the number to complete the sentence.

_____
_ _ _ _

It took _____ seconds for Joy's motorcycle to go down the ramp
10 times.

**You found evidence! Use the number you wrote to help you find a
clue on page 201.**

Two Equal Shares

Circle the shapes that are divided into two equal halves. Draw an **X** through shapes that are divided into unequal parts.

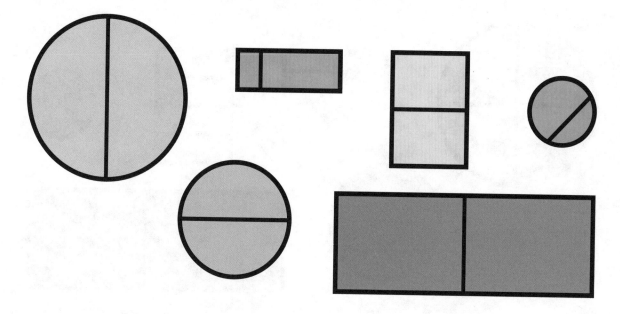

Draw a line to divide each food item into equal halves.

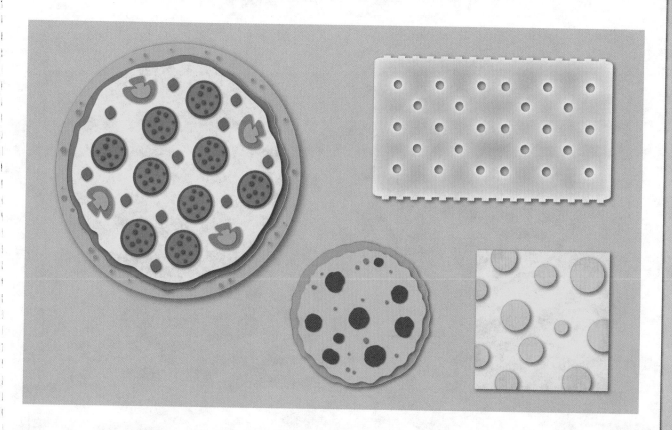

Four Equal Shares

Circle the shapes that are divided into equal fourths. Draw an **X** through shapes that are divided into unequal parts.

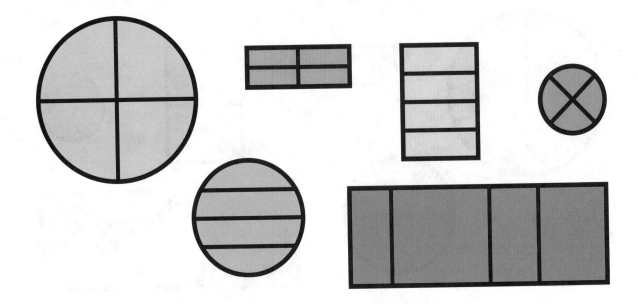

Draw a line to divide each food item into equal fourths.

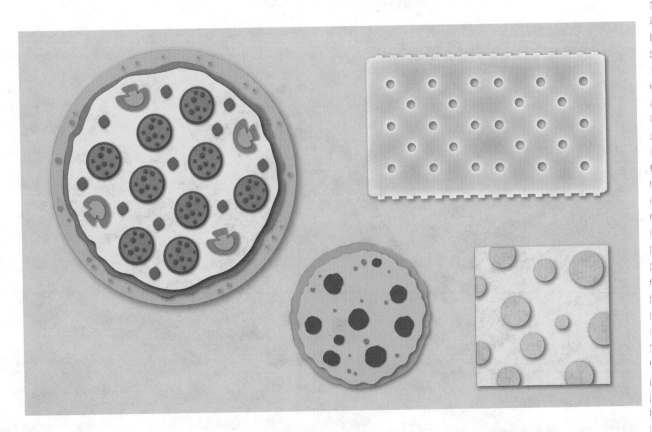

CLUE CORNER

Find the Keys

It is time to find a clue about "Escape from Room Eight"!

"Did you move the ramp in front of Hattie's cage this week?" asked Flynn.

"Yes," said Joy. "Last week it was behind the cage. This table is too crowded!"

"Do the vehicles ever hit the cage?" asked Flynn.

"I guess so. We can find out," said Joy as she launched the motorcycle down the ramp.

The little cycle flew right into Hattie's cage. Its handlebars got caught in the bars. What part of Hattie's cage did the motorcycle hit? To find out, solve the problems. Circle the answers that match the numbers you collected as evidence on pages 165, 175, 187, and 198.

Unscramble the letters on the keys next to the numbers you circled. Write a word to finish the sentence and find a clue.

Clue: What part of Hattie's cage did Joy's vehicles hit?

—— —— —— ——

— — — — — — — — — —

They hit the cage ——— ——— ——— ———.

Write the clue word you found in the Detective's Notebook on pages 202 and 203.

ESCAPE
FROM
ROOM EIGHT
Detective's
Notebook

When did the hamster escape?
(See page 8.)

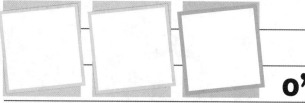

o'clock

Where was the hamster cage?
(See page 8.)

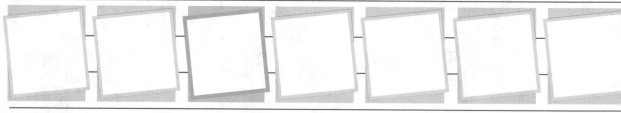

center

How could Hattie escape from her cage?
(See page 58.)

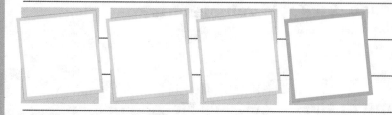

Name

ESCAPE
FROM
ROOM EIGHT
**Detective's
Notebook**

Who DID IT?

G. Whiz: What was the position of the robot's arm?
(See page 106.)

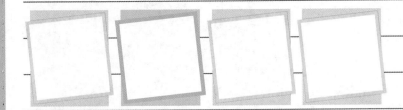

Pete Petty: Why did Pete think Hattie was safe?
(See page 154.)

Joy Ride: What part of Hattie's cage did Joy's vehicles hit?
(See page 201.)

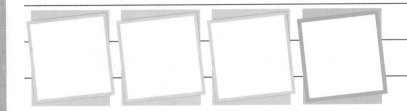

Use the letters in green boxes in your **Detective's Notebook** in order. Circle those letters to make choices and finish the story. You did it, first grade investigator! You solved the case!

Escape from Room Eight, conclusion

The students in room eight were putting papers away. School was almost over. Ms. Minder called Flynn Frunt into the hallway. "I hope you found some answers," she said.

"I did!" began Flynn. "First, I inspected the cage. The walls, floors, and roof are tight. I did not find any way for Hattie to get out by herself."

D. "The cage is old," said Ms. Minder. "We may need a new one."

E. "Good thinking," said Ms. Minder. "I am glad you checked."

F. "I had to fix the cage last year," said Ms. Minder. "It could be broken again."

"Someone or something must be opening the door from the outside," explained Flynn. "It could be Joy Ride. She moved her ramp in front of the cage. When motorcycles go down the ramp, they hit the door. The handlebars get stuck near the latch."

G. "That might be it," said Ms. Minder. "Do you have any other ideas?"

H. "Good work," said Ms. Minder. "That must be it! I will talk to Joy."

I. "It could not be Joy," said Ms. Minder. "Toy vehicles are not heavy enough to undo the latch."

"It could be Pete Petty," offered Flynn. "He may not latch the door when he puts Hattie back in her cage. He did not think she could jump down!"

L. "Good work," said Ms. Minder. "That must be it! I will talk to Pete."

M. "That might be it," said Ms. Minder. "Do you have any other ideas?"

N. "It could not be Pete," said Ms. Minder. "After he does experiments with Hattie, I make sure the cage door is latched. I will remind him that Hattie can jump!"

"It could be G. Whiz," tried Flynn. "His robot's timer makes the arm go down at one o'clock. That is right after recess! The robot is near the cage. Its arm could open the latch."

O. "Good work," said Ms. Minder. "That must be it! I did not know the robot had a timer."

P. "That might be it," said Ms. Minder. "Do you have any other ideas?"

Q. "It could not be G.," said Ms. Minder. "The timer is set for one o'clock in the morning, not one o'clock in the afternoon."

"We have another problem," said Flynn. "The science center is crowded. Kids cannot find space to work."

T. "I am afraid there is no more room," said Ms. Minder.

U. "Good point," said Ms. Minder. "We need another table in the science center. I will ask the principal to find one."

V. "Some students will have to put their projects away," said Ms. Minder.

"I am glad to hear that," said Flynn.

Q. "Hattie will be happier with more space," he said.

R. "Because I have an idea for a science project. By the way, do we have room for a guinea pig cage?" he asked.

S. "Maybe there will be room for Joy's cars, G.'s robot, and Hattie to race!" he joked.

"Hmm...we will see about that," said Ms. Minder. "I do know one thing. You are a clever investigator, Flynn Frunt. Thanks for solving the mystery in room eight!"

"You are welcome," said Flynn. "Let me know the next time there is a case to crack!"

ANSWER KEY

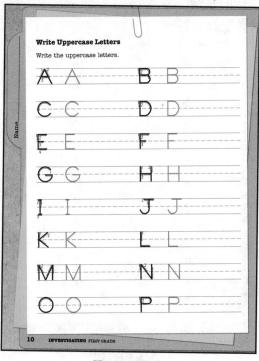

Page 10

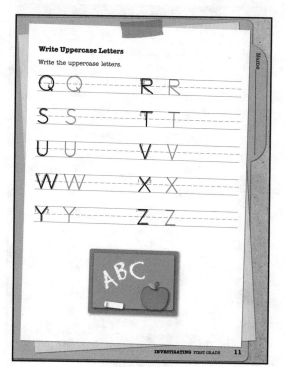

Page 11

Page 12

Page 13

ANSWER KEY

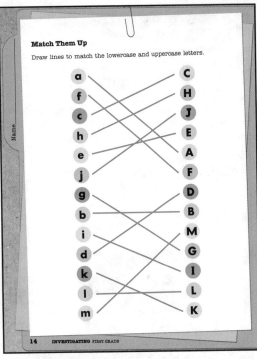

Page 14

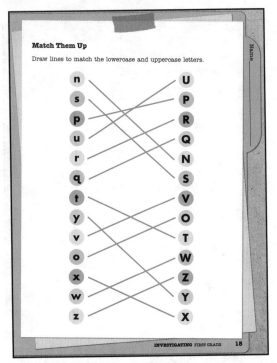

Page 15

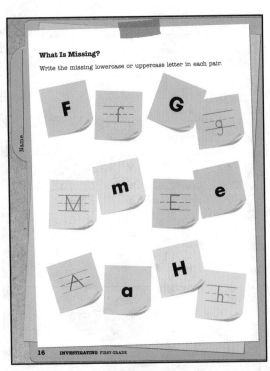

Page 16

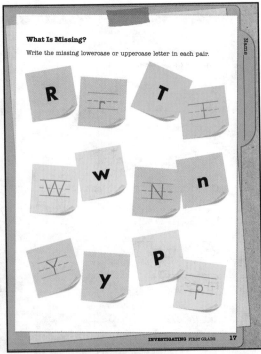

Page 17

Page 18

Page 19

Page 20

Page 21

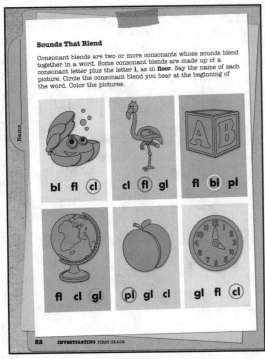

Page 22

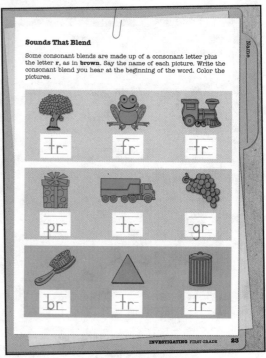

Page 23

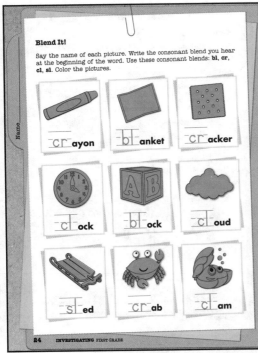

Page 24

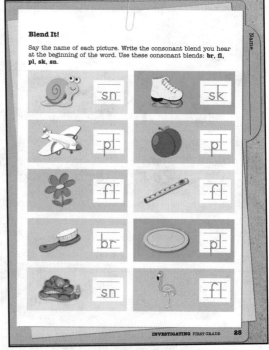

Page 25

They Begin with a Blend

Write a word that begins with a consonant blend to complete each sentence. Then, draw a picture to show each sentence.

sting	prize	drank	plant	stamp

Tom ___drank___ his water.

A bee can ___sting___ you.

I put a ___stamp___ on my letter.

The ___plant___ is green.

My story won first ___prize___.

Drawings will vary.

26 INVESTIGATING FIRST GRADE

Page 26

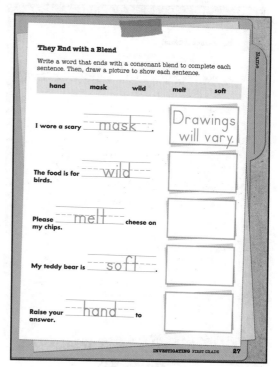

They End with a Blend

Write a word that ends with a consonant blend to complete each sentence. Then, draw a picture to show each sentence.

hand	mask	wild	melt	soft

I wore a scary ___mask___.

The food is for ___wild___ birds.

Please ___melt___ cheese on my chips.

My teddy bear is ___soft___.

Raise your ___hand___ to answer.

Drawings will vary.

INVESTIGATING FIRST GRADE 27

Page 27

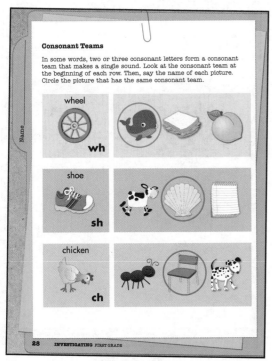

Consonant Teams

In some words, two or three consonant letters form a consonant team that makes a single sound. Look at the consonant team at the beginning of each row. Then, say the name of each picture. Circle the picture that has the same consonant team.

wheel — **wh**

shoe — **sh**

chicken — **ch**

28 INVESTIGATING FIRST GRADE

Page 28

Consonant Teams

Look at the consonant team at the beginning of each row. Then, say the name of each picture. Circle the picture that has the same consonant team.

duck — **ck**

ring — **ng**

tooth — **th**

INVESTIGATING FIRST GRADE 29

Page 29

ANSWER KEY

Go Consonant Team!

Write a word with a consonant team to complete each sentence.

shut	chain	patch	which	splash

My bike **chain** is loose.

Which sticker do you want?

Please **shut** the door.

Use a **patch** to cover the hole.

We like to **splash** in the tub.

30 INVESTIGATING FIRST GRADE

Page 30

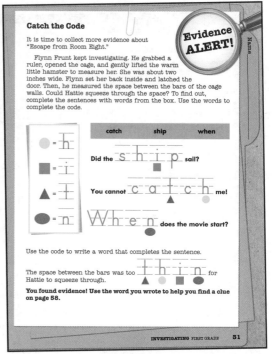

Catch the Code

Evidence ALERT!

It is time to collect more evidence about "Escape from Room Eight."

Flynn Frunt kept investigating. He grabbed a ruler, opened the cage, and gently lifted the warm little hamster to measure her. She was about two inches wide. Flynn set her back inside and latched the door. Then, he measured the space between the bars of the cage walls. Could Hattie squeeze through the space? To find out, complete the sentences with words from the box. Use the words to complete the code.

catch	ship	when

● = h
■ = i
▲ = t
⬤ = n

Did the **ship** ■ sail?

You cannot **catch** ▲ ⬤ me!

When ⬤ does the movie start?

Use the code to write a word that completes the sentence.

The space between the bars was too **thin** ▲ ⬤ ■ ⬤ for Hattie to squeeze through.

You found evidence! Use the word you wrote to help you find a clue on page 58.

INVESTIGATING FIRST GRADE 31

Page 31

The Sound of Short a

Short a is the middle sound in the word **rat**. Say the name of each picture. Then, spell each word by writing a consonant for the beginning sound, **a** for the **short a** sound in the middle, and a consonant for the ending sound. Color the pictures.

map   bat

fan   ham

32 INVESTIGATING FIRST GRADE

Page 32

The Sound of Long a

Long a says its name. It is the vowel sound you hear in the word **same**. Say each word. Color the pictures for words that have the **long a** sound.

cake   frog

train   tree

grapes   crab

INVESTIGATING FIRST GRADE 33

Page 33

Page 34

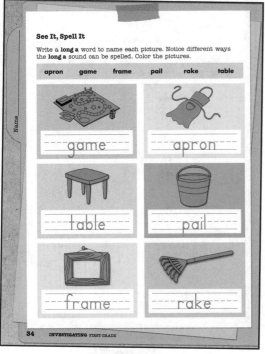

See It, Spell It

Write a **long a** word to name each picture. Notice different ways the **long a** sound can be spelled. Color the pictures.

apron	game	frame	pail	rake	table

game | apron

table | pail

frame | rake

34 INVESTIGATING FIRST GRADE

Page 34

Page 35

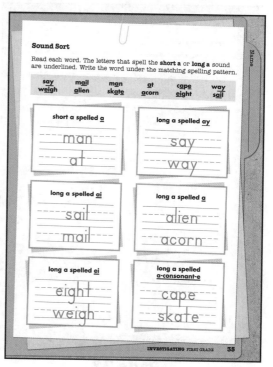

Sound Sort

Read each word. The letters that spell the **short a** or **long a** sound are underlined. Write the word under the matching spelling pattern.

say weigh	mail alien	man skate	at acorn	cape eight	way sail

short a spelled a
man
at

long a spelled ay
say
way

long a spelled ai
sail
mail

long a spelled a
alien
acorn

long a spelled ei
eight
weigh

long a spelled a-consonant-e
cape
skate

INVESTIGATING FIRST GRADE 35

Page 35

Page 36

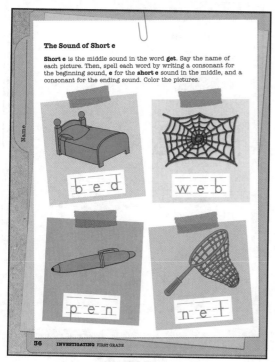

The Sound of Short e

Short e is the middle sound in the word **get**. Say the name of each picture. Then, spell each word by writing a consonant for the beginning sound, **e** for the **short e** sound in the middle, and a consonant for the ending sound. Color the pictures.

b e d | w e b

p e n | n e t

36 INVESTIGATING FIRST GRADE

Page 36

Page 37

The Sound of Long e

Long e says its name. It is the vowel sound you hear in the word **seat**. Say each word. Color the pictures for words that have the **long e** sound.

feet

fish

tree

seal

tent

leaf

INVESTIGATING FIRST GRADE 37

Page 37

ANSWER KEY

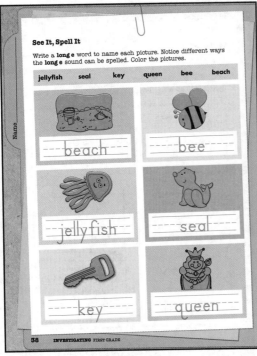

Page 38

Page 39

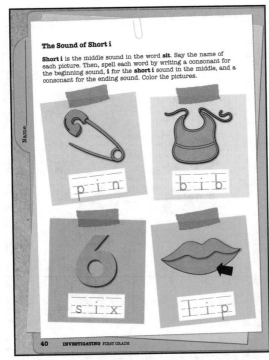

Page 40

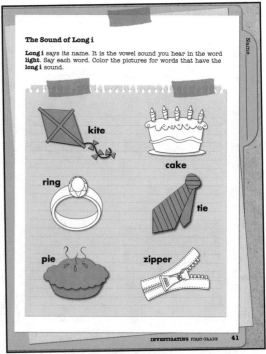

Page 41

214 **INVESTIGATING** FIRST GRADE

Page 42

See It, Spell It

Write a **long i** word to name each picture. Notice different ways the **long i** sound can be spelled. Color the pictures.

five	pie	dinosaur	fire	slide	mice

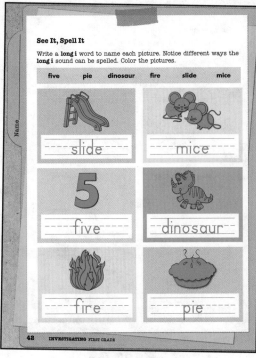

slide

mice

five

dinosaur

fire

pie

Page 43

Spelling Spy

Evidence ALERT!

It is time to collect more evidence about "Escape from Room Eight."

Flynn Frunt watched Hattie walk to the glass water bottle hanging on the side of the cage. Maybe, Flynn thought, Hattie could climb on top of the bottle and escape through the roof. Hattie drank from the bottle with her little pink tongue. Then, she stretched her front paws up the side of the bottle and tried to climb. What happened? To find out, write the **long i** word that matches each spelling clue.

invite	shy	pie	light

If you can spell **dry**, then you can spell _shy_.

If you can spell **night**, then you can spell _light_.

If you can spell **white**, then you can spell _invite_.

If you can spell **tie**, then you can spell _pie_.

Now, write the first letter of each word you wrote, in order, to make a word that completes the sentence.

The smooth glass water bottle made Hattie's paws

s l i p

You found evidence! Use the word you wrote to help you find a clue on page 58.

Page 44

The Sound of Short o

Short o is the middle sound in the word **got**. Say the name of each picture. Then, spell each word by writing a consonant for the beginning sound, **o** for the **short o** sound in the middle, and a consonant for the ending sound. Color the pictures.

box

dog

top

log

Page 45

The Sound of Long o

Long o says its name. It is the vowel sound you hear in the word **go**. Say each word. Color the pictures for words that have the **long o** sound.

goat

lock

yo-yo

deer

coat

globe

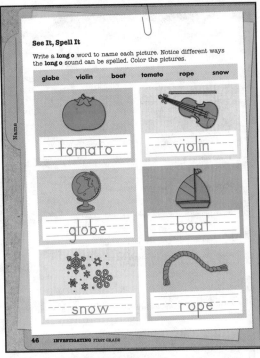

Page 46

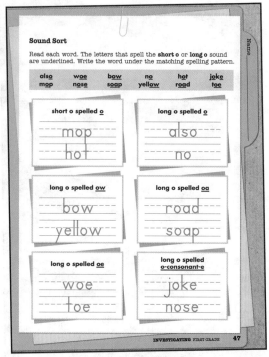

Page 47

Page 48

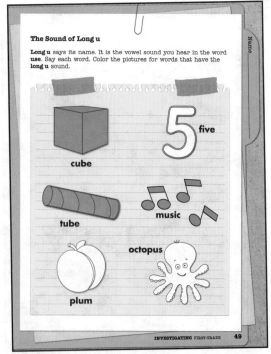

Page 49

ANSWER KEY

See It, Spell It

Write a **long u** word to name each picture. Notice different ways the **long u** sound can be spelled. Color the pictures.

unicycle	glue	cube	flute	tube	unicorn

flute

unicorn

glue

unicycle

tube

cube

50   INVESTIGATING FIRST GRADE

Page 50

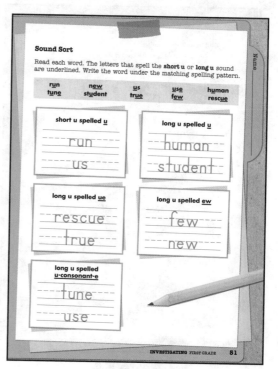

Sound Sort

Read each word. The letters that spell the **short u** or **long u** sound are underlined. Write the word under the matching spelling pattern.

r<u>u</u>n	n<u>ew</u>	<u>u</u>s	<u>u</u>s<u>e</u>	h<u>u</u>man
t<u>u</u>ne	st<u>u</u>dent	tr<u>ue</u>	f<u>ew</u>	resc<u>ue</u>

short u spelled <u>u</u>
run
us

long u spelled <u>u</u>
human
student

long u spelled <u>ue</u>
rescue
true

long u spelled <u>ew</u>
few
new

long u spelled u-consonant-e
tune
use

INVESTIGATING FIRST GRADE   51

Page 51

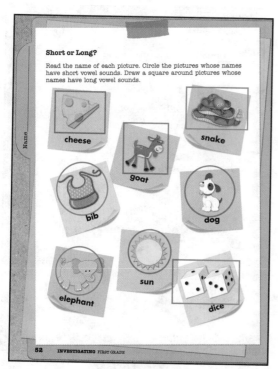

Short or Long?

Read the name of each picture. Circle the pictures whose names have short vowel sounds. Draw a square around pictures whose names have long vowel sounds.

cheese

snake

goat

bib

dog

elephant

sun

dice

52   INVESTIGATING FIRST GRADE

Page 52

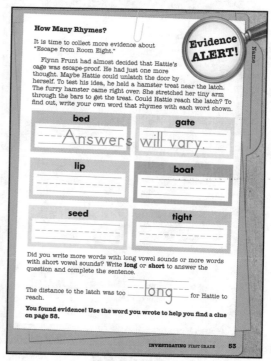

How Many Rhymes?

It is time to collect more evidence about "Escape from Room Eight."

Flynn Frunt had almost decided that Hattie's cage was escape-proof. He had just one more thought. Maybe Hattie could unlatch the door by herself. To test his idea, he held a hamster treat near the latch. The furry hamster came right over. She stretched her tiny arm through the bars to get the treat. Could Hattie reach the latch? To find out, write your own word that rhymes with each word shown.

Evidence ALERT!

bed	gate
Answers	will vary.

lip	boat

seed	tight

Did you write more words with long vowel sounds or more words with short vowel sounds? Write **long** or **short** to answer the question and complete the sentence.

The distance to the latch was too ___long___ for Hattie to reach.

You found evidence! Use the word you wrote to help you find a clue on page 58.

INVESTIGATING FIRST GRADE   53

Page 53

INVESTIGATING FIRST GRADE   **217**

ANSWER KEY

Page 54

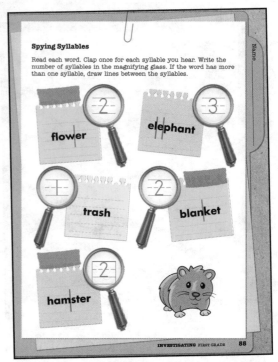

Page 55

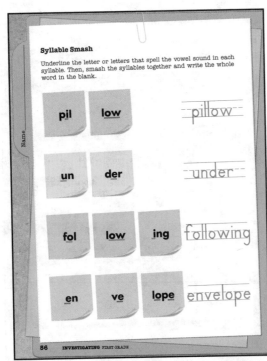

Page 56

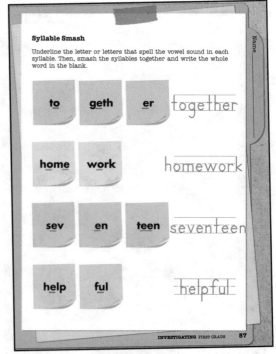

Page 57

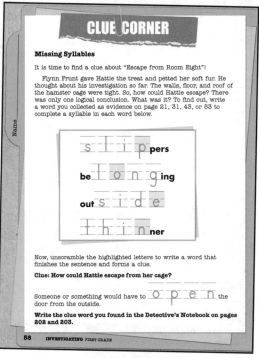

Page 58

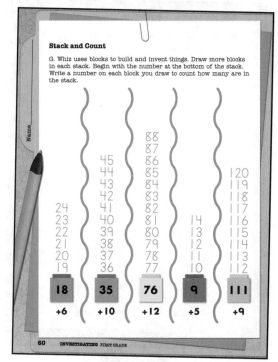

Page 60

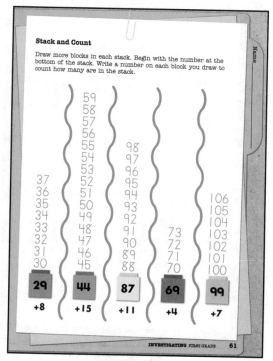

Page 61

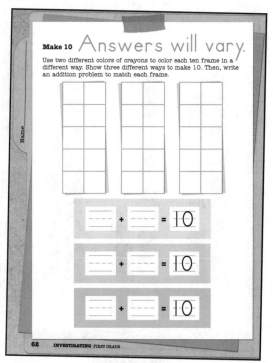

Page 62

Make 10 — Answers will vary.

Use two different colors of crayons to color each ten frame in a different way. Show three different ways to make 10. Then, write an addition problem to match each frame.

Page 63

10 Plus Some

Add the yellow blocks to each stack of 10 red blocks. Write the sum.

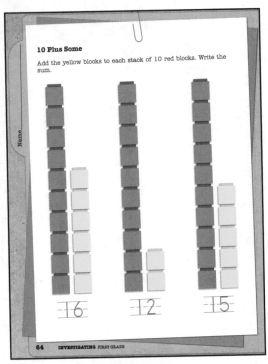

Page 64

10 Plus Some

Add the green blocks to each stack of 10 red blocks. Write the sum.

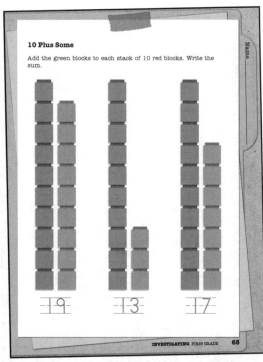

Page 65

Frame Game

The first frame in each pair shows 10. Color boxes in the second frame in each pair to show the number.

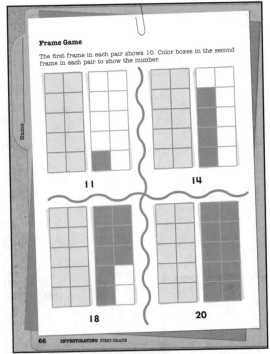

Page 66

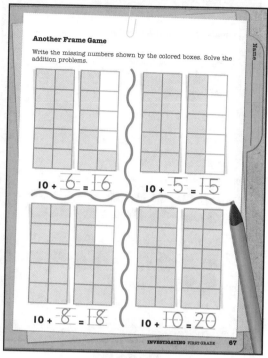

Page 67

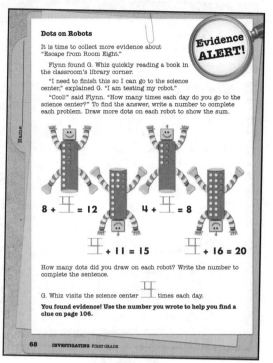

Page 68

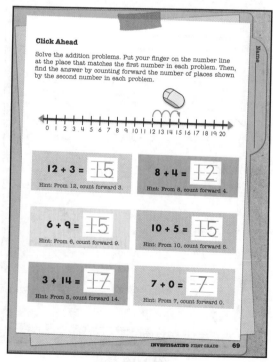

Page 69

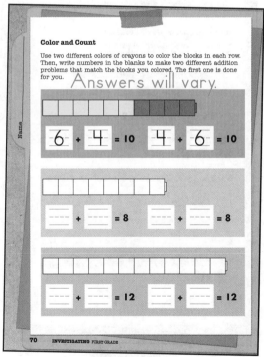

Page 70

ANSWER KEY

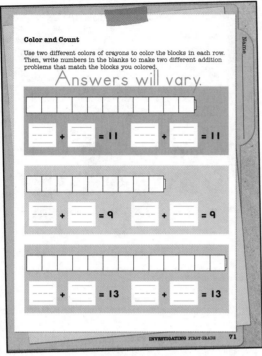

Color and Count

Use two different colors of crayons to color the blocks in each row. Then, write numbers in the blanks to make two different addition problems that match the blocks you colored.

Answers will vary.

___ + ___ = 11   ___ + ___ = 11

___ + ___ = 9   ___ + ___ = 9

___ + ___ = 13   ___ + ___ = 13

INVESTIGATING FIRST GRADE 71

Page 71

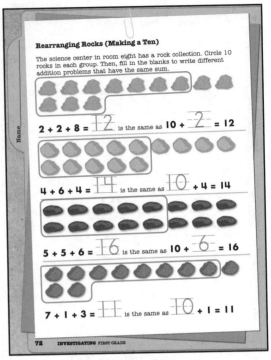

Rearranging Rocks (Making a Ten)

The science center in room eight has a rock collection. Circle 10 rocks in each group. Then, fill in the blanks to write different addition problems that have the same sum.

2 + 2 + 8 = 12 is the same as 10 + 2 = 12

4 + 6 + 4 = 14 is the same as 10 + 4 = 14

5 + 5 + 6 = 16 is the same as 10 + 6 = 16

7 + 1 + 3 = 11 is the same as 10 + 1 = 11

72 INVESTIGATING FIRST GRADE

Page 72

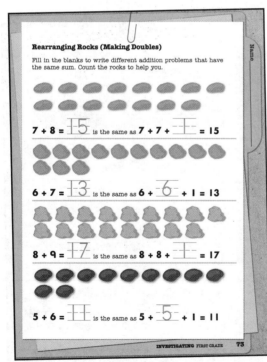

Rearranging Rocks (Making Doubles)

Fill in the blanks to write different addition problems that have the same sum. Count the rocks to help you.

7 + 8 = 15 is the same as 7 + 7 + 1 = 15

6 + 7 = 13 is the same as 6 + 6 + 1 = 13

8 + 9 = 17 is the same as 8 + 8 + 1 = 17

5 + 6 = 11 is the same as 5 + 5 + 1 = 11

INVESTIGATING FIRST GRADE 73

Page 73

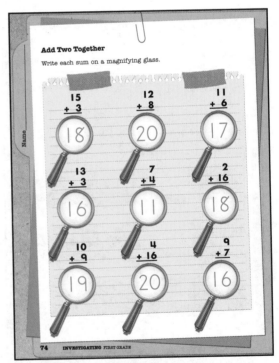

Add Two Together

Write each sum on a magnifying glass.

15 + 3 = 18   12 + 8 = 20   11 + 6 = 17

13 + 3 = 16   7 + 4 = 11   2 + 16 = 18

10 + 9 = 19   4 + 16 = 20   9 + 7 = 16

74 INVESTIGATING FIRST GRADE

Page 74

Page 75

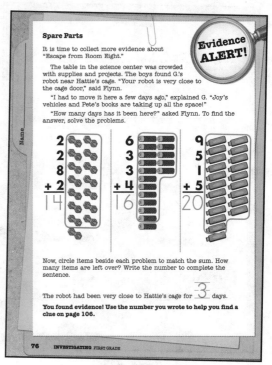

Page 76

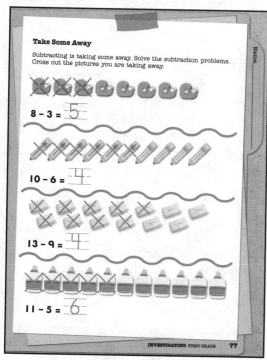

Page 77

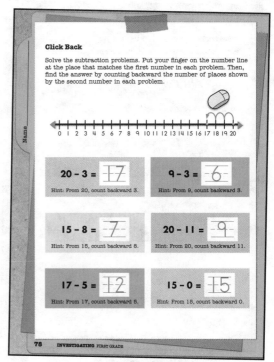

Page 78

ANSWER KEY

Click Back

Solve the subtraction problems. Put your finger on the number line at the place that matches the first number in each problem. Then, find the answer by counting backward the number of places shown by the second number in each problem.

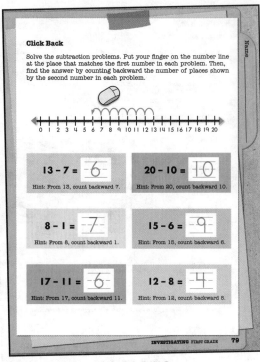

13 − 7 = 6
Hint: From 13, count backward 7.

20 − 10 = 10
Hint: From 20, count backward 10.

8 − 1 = 7
Hint: From 8, count backward 1.

15 − 6 = 9
Hint: From 15, count backward 6.

17 − 11 = 6
Hint: From 17, count backward 11.

12 − 8 = 4
Hint: From 12, count backward 8.

Page 79

Thinking Machine

First, solve each addition problem. Use the sum to help you solve the subtraction problem.

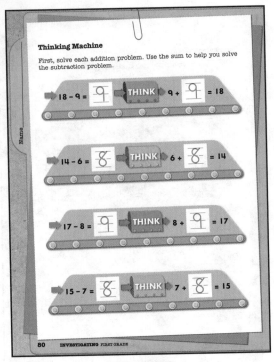

18 − 9 = 9   THINK   9 + 9 = 18

14 − 6 = 8   THINK   6 + 8 = 14

17 − 8 = 9   THINK   8 + 9 = 17

15 − 7 = 8   THINK   7 + 8 = 15

Page 80

Thinking Machine

First, solve each addition problem. Use the sum to help you solve the subtraction problem.

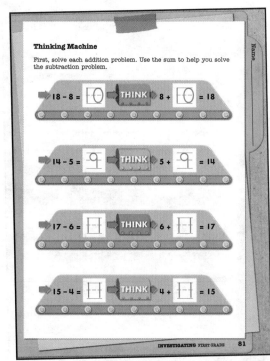

18 − 8 = 10   THINK   8 + 10 = 18

14 − 5 = 9   THINK   5 + 9 = 14

17 − 6 = 11   THINK   6 + 11 = 17

15 − 4 = 11   THINK   4 + 11 = 15

Page 81

Subtraction Squares

Subtract each row and then each column. Write the answers on the lines.

11 6 5
3 2 1
8 4 4

14 7 7
5 4 1
9 3 6

16 8 8
9 4 5
7 4 3

Page 82

Page 83

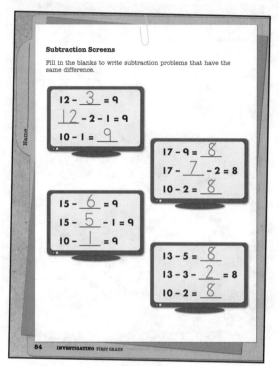

Page 84

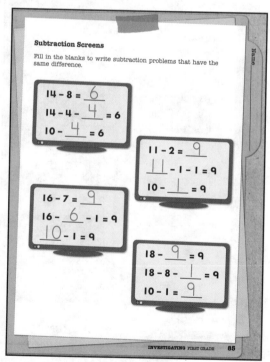

Page 85

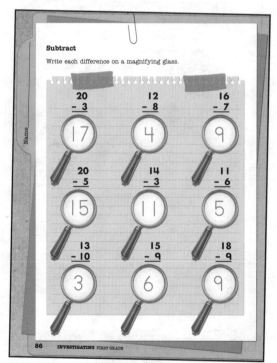

Page 86

Page 87

Page 88

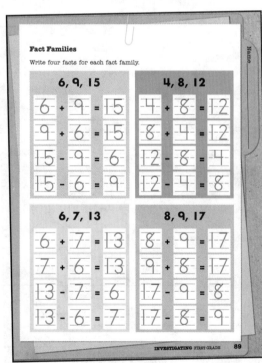

Page 89

Page 90

Page 91

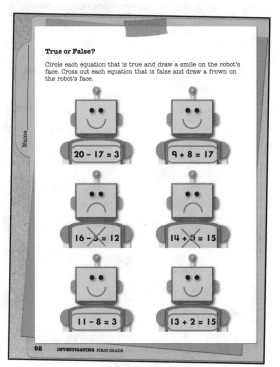

Page 92

Page 93

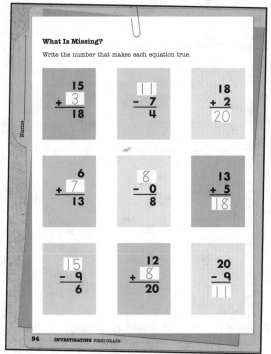

Page 94

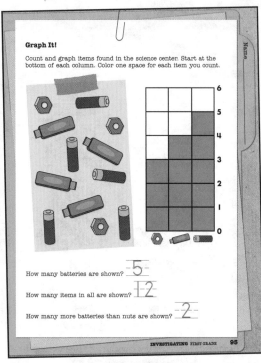

Page 95

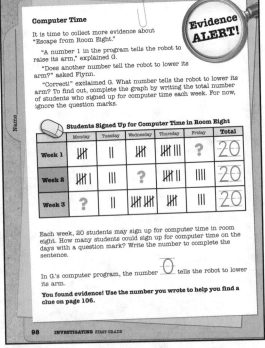

Page 96

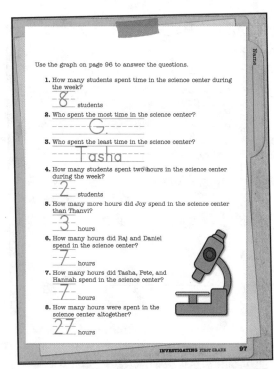

Page 97

Page 95

Graph It!

Count and graph items found in the science center. Start at the bottom of each column. Color one space for each item you count.

How many batteries are shown? 5

How many items in all are shown? 12

How many more batteries than nuts are shown? 2

Page 96

Science Center Students

Ms. Minder made a picture graph to show how much time students in room eight spent in the science center during one week.

Student	Hours Spent in Science Center
Raj	(3 microscopes)
Joy	(5 microscopes)
Tasha	(1 microscope)
Pete	(4 microscopes)
Hannah	(2 microscopes)
G.	(6 microscopes)
Thanvi	(2 microscopes)
Daniel	(4 microscopes)

= one hour spent in science center

Page 97

Use the graph on page 96 to answer the questions.

1. How many students spent time in the science center during the week?
8 students

2. Who spent the most time in the science center?
G.

3. Who spent the least time in the science center?
Tasha

4. How many students spent two hours in the science center during the week?
2 students

5. How many more hours did Joy spend in the science center than Thanvi?
3 hours

6. How many hours did Raj and Daniel spend in the science center?
7 hours

7. How many hours did Tasha, Pete, and Hannah spend in the science center?
7 hours

8. How many hours were spent in the science center altogether?
27 hours

Page 98

Computer Time

Evidence ALERT!

It is time to collect more evidence about "Escape from Room Eight."

"A number 1 in the program tells the robot to raise its arm," explained G.

"Does another number tell the robot to lower its arm?" asked Flynn.

"Correct!" exclaimed G. What number tells the robot to lower its arm? To find out, complete the graph by writing the total number of students who signed up for computer time each week. For now, ignore the question marks.

	Students Signed Up for Computer Time in Room Eight					
	Monday	Tuesday	Wednesday	Thursday	Friday	Total
Week 1	卌	‖	卌	卌 ‖‖	?	20
Week 2	卌	‖‖	?	卌	‖‖‖	20
Week 3	?	‖	卌 卌	卌	‖‖	20

Each week, 20 students may sign up for computer time in room eight. How many students could sign up for computer time on the days with a question mark? Write the number to complete the sentence.

In G.'s computer program, the number 0 tells the robot to lower its arm.

You found evidence! Use the number you wrote to help you find a clue on page 106.

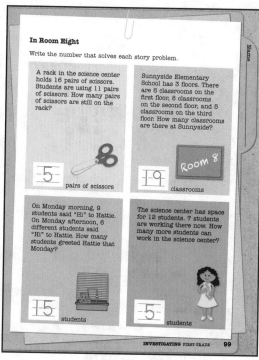

Page 99

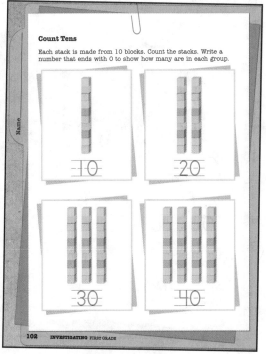

Page 100

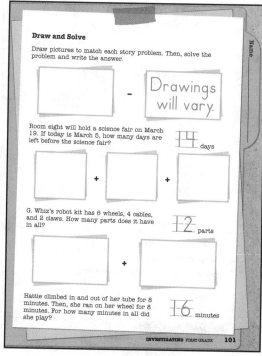

Page 101

Page 102

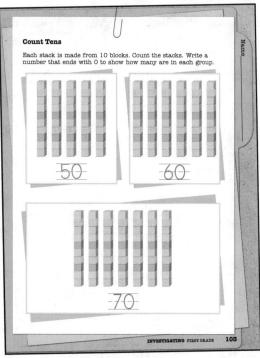

Page 103

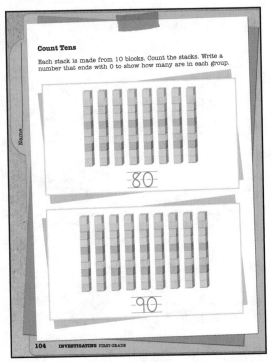

Page 104

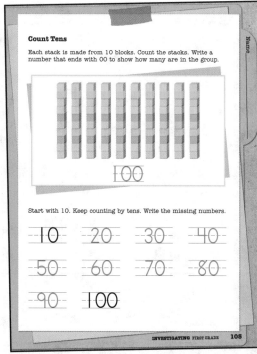

Page 105

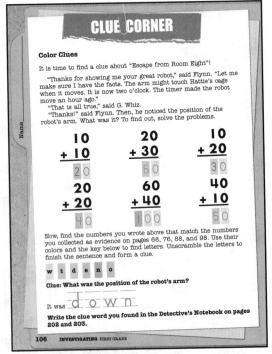

Page 106

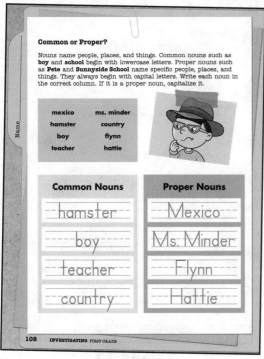

Page 108

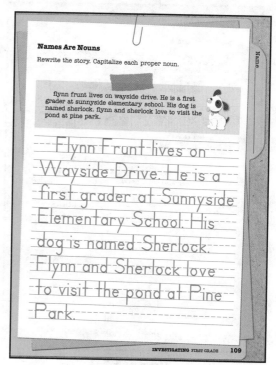

Page 109

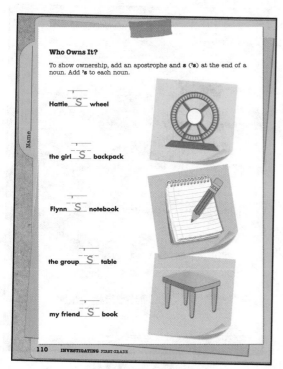

Page 110

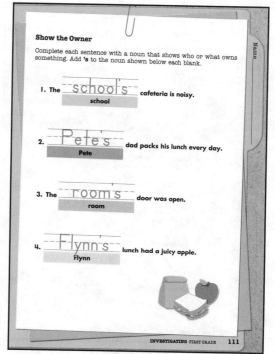

Page 111

Noun-Verb Match

When a sentence tells about something that is happening right now, look at the noun in the sentence. If it names one person, place, or thing, the matching verb often ends with **s**. (Example: Flynn **looks** around.) If the noun is plural, the verb often does not end with **s**. (Example: The students **work**.) Circle a verb to complete each sentence. Write it in the blank.

1. The students in room eight _eat_ lunch before recess.
   eats (**eat**)

2. Flynn _leads_ the class back to room eight at one o'clock.
   (**leads**) lead

3. Hattie often _runs_ on her wheel.
   (**runs**) run

4. G. Whiz, Pete Petty, and Joy Ride _visit_ the science center a lot.
   visits (**visit**)

5. Ms. Minder _helps_ the students with their science projects.
   (**helps**) help

Page 112

It Is Happening Now

When a sentence tells about something that is happening right now, use a present-tense verb. Circle the sentences that tell what is happening now. Underline the verb in each sentence you circle.

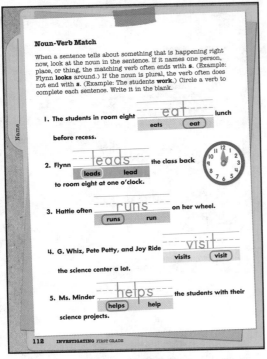

Flynn <u>wants</u> to know all the facts.

Hattie escaped three times.

The students <u>love</u> their pet Hattie.

Ms. Minder will try to fix the problem.

Pete <u>reads</u> lots of books about animals.

Page 113

It Already Happened

When a sentence tells about something that already happened, use a past-tense verb. Circle the sentences that tell what already happened. Underline the verb in each sentence you circle.

Hamsters love to crawl in tubes.

Hattie <u>escaped</u> three times.

Hamsters will hide when they are frightened.

Hattie <u>jumped</u> off the science center table.

The class pet <u>ran</u> into the hallway.

Page 114

It Will Happen

When a sentence tells about something that will happen, use a future-tense verb. Circle the sentences that tell what will happen. Underline the verb in each sentence you circle.

Pete filled Hattie's food dish.

The students <u>will</u> try to keep Hattie safe.

Pete <u>will close</u> the cage door tightly.

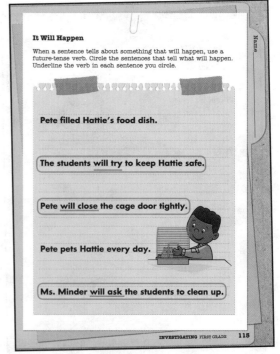

Pete pets Hattie every day.

Ms. Minder <u>will ask</u> the students to clean up.

Page 115

Verb Tense Test

Evidence ALERT!

It is time to collect more evidence about "Escape from Room Eight."

Pete Petty stood near the cage. "May I ask you some questions?" said Flynn.

"Sure," said Pete. "You want to know about me and Hattie, right?"

"I know you like to take care of her," said Flynn.

"I do! I love animals," explained Pete. "I brush her and pet her. Every week, I bring something from home for her." What does Pete bring? To find out, write a verb in each sentence that matches the tense shown.

brought	f<u>ee</u>d	foun<u>d</u>	will la<u>t</u>ch

1. The students **will latch** Hattie's cage tightly from now on.
   Future Tense

2. Flynn **found** Hattie running into the hallway.
   Past Tense

3. Pete **brought** something for Hattie last week.
   Past Tense

4. It is a student's job to **feed** Hattie every day.
   Present Tense

Find the underlined letters in the verbs you wrote. Write them, in order, in the blanks to make a word that completes the sentence.

Every week, Pete brings Hattie a cardboard **t u b e**

You found evidence! Use the word you wrote to help you find a clue on page 154.

116   INVESTIGATING FIRST GRADE

Page 116

Personal Pronouns

A pronoun takes the place of a noun. Write a pronoun that could take the place of each underlined noun.

she	it	they	he

1. <u>Ms. Minder</u> frowned. **She** was worried about Hattie.

2. First, <u>the students</u> in room eight have lunch. Then, **they** go to recess.

3. <u>Flynn</u> thought for a while. **He** had an idea.

4. There is a <u>robot</u> in the science center. **It** has an arm that goes up and down.

5. <u>Pete and Flynn</u> played at recess. **They** played on the swings.

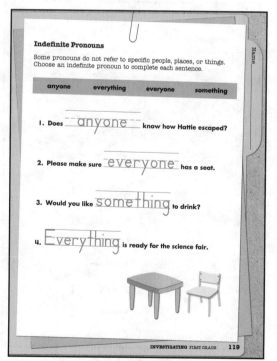

INVESTIGATING FIRST GRADE   117

Page 117

Possessive Pronouns

Possessive pronouns show ownership. Complete each sentence with a possessive pronoun that matches the underlined pronoun.

her	its	his	my	their

1. <u>It</u> has a plastic floor. **Its** walls are metal bars.

2. <u>She</u> rides bus 42. **Her** bus arrives at 8:40.

3. <u>They</u> are working on science projects. **Their** projects are almost done.

4. <u>He</u> has many questions. Will **his** questions be answered?

5. <u>I</u> am a student in room eight. **My** class has a pet hamster.

118   INVESTIGATING FIRST GRADE

Page 118

Indefinite Pronouns

Some pronouns do not refer to specific people, places, or things. Choose an indefinite pronoun to complete each sentence.

anyone	everything	everyone	something

1. Does **anyone** know how Hattie escaped?

2. Please make sure **everyone** has a seat.

3. Would you like **something** to drink?

4. **Everything** is ready for the science fair.

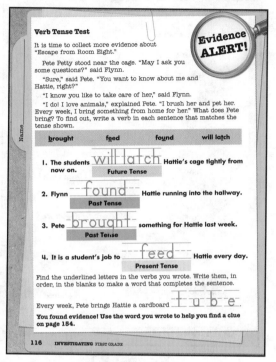

INVESTIGATING FIRST GRADE   119

Page 119

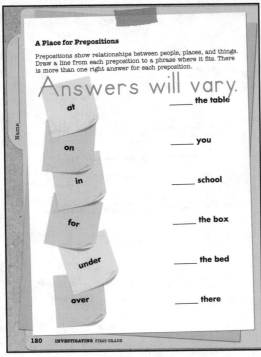

A Place for Prepositions

Prepositions show relationships between people, places, and things. Draw a line from each preposition to a phrase where it fits. There is more than one right answer for each preposition.

Name

Answers will vary.

at   _____ the table

on   _____ you

in   _____ school

for   _____ the box

under   _____ the bed

over   _____ there

120 INVESTIGATING FIRST GRADE

Page 120

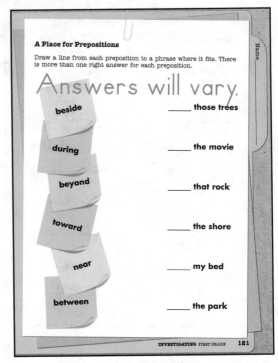

A Place for Prepositions

Draw a line from each preposition to a phrase where it fits. There is more than one right answer for each preposition.

Name

Answers will vary.

beside   _____ those trees

during   _____ the movie

beyond   _____ that rock

toward   _____ the shore

near   _____ my bed

between   _____ the park

INVESTIGATING FIRST GRADE 121

Page 121

In the Science Center

For each number, write a preposition that describes where something is in the science center.

Name

| against | beside | under | near |

Science Center

Answers will vary. Possible answers shown.

1. against the cage
2. beside   the computer
3. under   the table
4. near   the edge

122 INVESTIGATING FIRST GRADE

Page 122

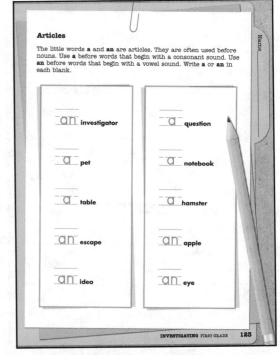

Articles

The little words **a** and **an** are articles. They are often used before nouns. Use **a** before words that begin with a consonant sound. Use **an** before words that begin with a vowel sound. Write **a** or **an** in each blank.

Name

an investigator   a question

a pet   a notebook

a table   a hamster

an escape   an apple

an idea   an eye

INVESTIGATING FIRST GRADE 123

Page 123

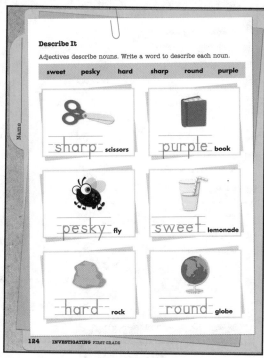

Page 124

Page 125

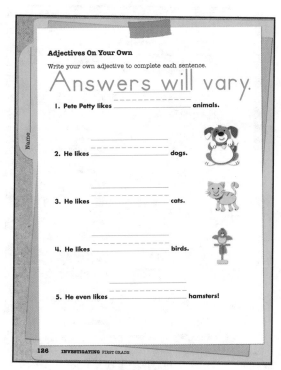

Page 126

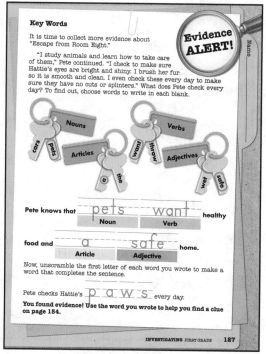

Page 127

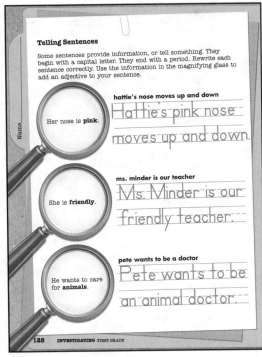

Page 128

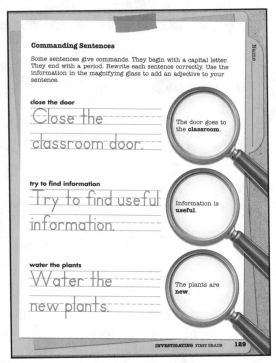

Page 129

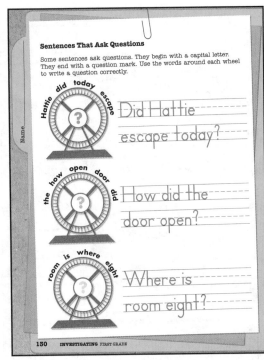

Page 130

Page 131

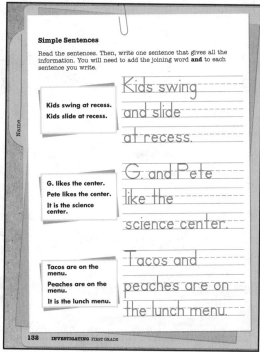

Page 132

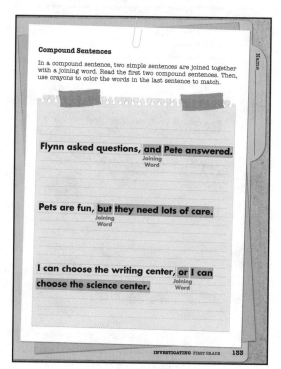

Page 133

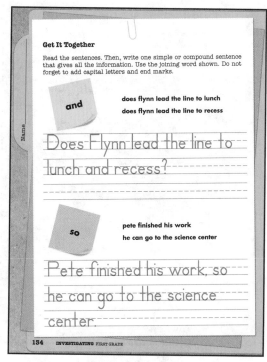

Page 134

Page 135

ANSWER KEY

Page 136

Words That Join

Joining words include **and**, **but**, **or**, **so**, and **yet**. Circle one or more joining words in each sentence.

Pete Petty is seven years old, (and) he goes to Sunnyside School.

At recess, Pete likes to climb (and) swing, (or) he likes to play foursquare.

Pete loves animals, (so) he has lots of books about them.

Pete often jokes around, (yet) he is a good student.

Pete likes mammals (and) reptiles, (but) he likes insects (and) birds, too.

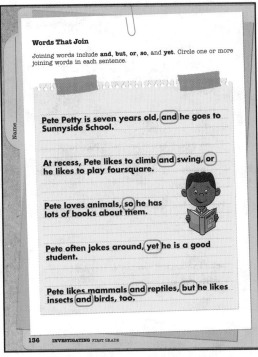

136 INVESTIGATING FIRST GRADE

Page 136

Page 137

Color Code

Evidence ALERT!

It is time to collect more evidence about "Escape from Room Eight."

"Hattie helps me do science experiments," said Pete. "I collect data about how much she eats each day. I want to find out if she eats more on days when students are at school than she does on weekends. I also take notes about how much time she spends doing this." What does Pete take notes about? To find out, write a joining word (**and**, **but**, **so**) to complete each sentence.

A hamster is smaller than a guinea pig, **but** it is larger than a mouse.

Joy's name is on the job chart, **so** it is her turn to feed Hattie.

Do not feed a hamster peanut butter **and** jelly.

Now, find one letter that is shared by all the words with the same color. Write the letters to find a word that completes the sentence.

Pete takes notes about how long Hattie **j o g s** on her wheel.

You found evidence! Use the word you wrote to help you find a clue on page 184.

INVESTIGATING FIRST GRADE 137

Page 137

Page 138

Add an Ending

Add endings to the verbs. Complete the chart. You may need to change the spelling of the base word before the ending is added. The first row is done for you.

	–s	–ed	–ing
work	works	worked	working
share	shares	shared	sharing
pet	pets	petted	petting
carry	carries	carried	carrying
stop	stops	stopped	stopping

138 INVESTIGATING FIRST GRADE

Page 138

Page 139

Paw Print Pairs

Choose a base word. Combine it with a prefix or a suffix from the paw prints to make a new word. You may need to change the spelling of the base word. Write the new words on the lines.

play	lock	do	take
match	lead	help	watch

Answers will vary. Possible answers shown.

mistake   unlock
watchful   helped
redo   leader

INVESTIGATING FIRST GRADE 139

Page 139

ANSWER KEY

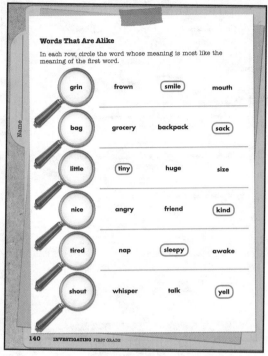

Words That Are Alike

In each row, circle the word whose meaning is most like the meaning of the first word.

grin	frown	(smile)	mouth
bag	grocery	backpack	(sack)
little	(tiny)	huge	size
nice	angry	friend	(kind)
tired	nap	(sleepy)	awake
shout	whisper	talk	(yell)

Page 140

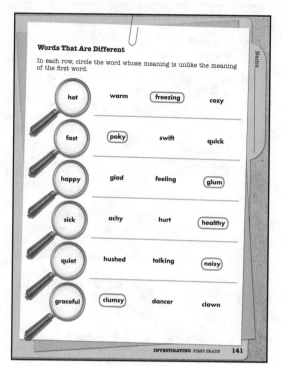

Words That Are Different

In each row, circle the word whose meaning is unlike the meaning of the first word.

hot	warm	(freezing)	cozy
fast	(poky)	swift	quick
happy	glad	feeling	(glum)
sick	achy	hurt	(healthy)
quiet	hushed	talking	(noisy)
graceful	(clumsy)	dancer	clown

Page 141

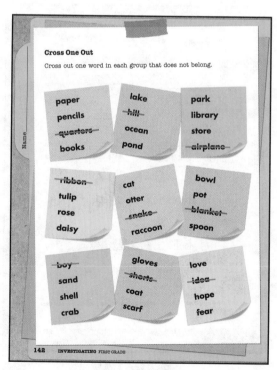

Cross One Out

Cross out one word in each group that does not belong.

paper
pencils
~~quarters~~
books

lake
~~hill~~
ocean
pond

park
library
store
~~airplane~~

~~ribbon~~
tulip
rose
daisy

cat
otter
~~snake~~
raccoon

bowl
pot
~~blanket~~
spoon

~~boy~~
sand
shell
crab

gloves
~~shorts~~
coat
scarf

love
~~idea~~
hope
fear

Page 142

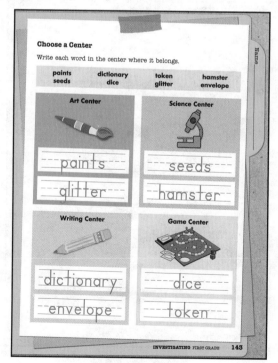

Choose a Center

Write each word in the center where it belongs.

paints   dictionary   token   hamster
seeds   dice   glitter envelope

Art Center
paints
glitter

Science Center
seeds
hamster

Writing Center
dictionary
envelope

Game Center
dice
token

Page 143

ANSWER KEY

Page 144

Many Meanings

In each pair of words, circle the word that has the stronger meaning.

- (scream) / say
- okay / (great)
- fall / (crash)
- close / (slam)
- (silky) / soft
- sip / (gulp)

In each pair of words, circle the word that has the weaker meaning.

- (nervous) / terrified
- exhausted / (sleepy)
- boiling / (hot)
- (small) / tiny
- sprint / (jog)
- (ask) / beg

Page 144

Page 145

Spell and Write

Circle the correctly spelled word to finish each sentence. Write it in the blank.

1. Please give this note ___to___ Flynn.
   two   toe   (to)

2. Are ___you___ in room eight?
   (you)   yoo   ewe

3. Ms. Minder ___was___ worried.
   (was)   wuz   waz

4. These supplies are ___from___ the science center.
   form   (from)   frum

5. ___There___ is Pete's experiment.
   Theer   Their   (There)

6. Write the answer on the ___board___.
   boord   (board)   bord

Page 145

Page 146

Spell and Write

Circle the correctly spelled word to finish each sentence. Write it in the blank.

1. Do you ___want___ to see Hattie?
   went   (want)   wunt

2. Ms. Minder helps us ___learn___.
   (learn)   lern   lurn

3. Can the robot ___move___ its arm?
   (move)   moov   muve

4. It is time to ___walk___ to the cafeteria.
   wok   (walk)   wock

5. The students ___were___ reading.
   where   (were)   wir

Page 146

Page 147

Follow the Path

Evidence ALERT!

It is time to collect more evidence about "Escape from Room Eight."

"Do you ever take Hattie out of her cage?" Flynn asked Pete.

"Well..." Pete began. "I have taken her out the past few days. But only for an important experiment! I built something special for her to run through. I use a timer to see how fast she goes." What did Pete build? To find out, draw a path through the letters needed to spell a word that completes the sentence.

It is not safe for Hattie to be ___outside___ of her cage.

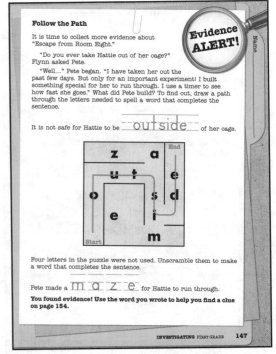

Four letters in the puzzle were not used. Unscramble them to make a word that completes the sentence.

Pete made a ___maze___ for Hattie to run through.

You found evidence! Use the word you wrote to help you find a clue on page 154.

Page 147

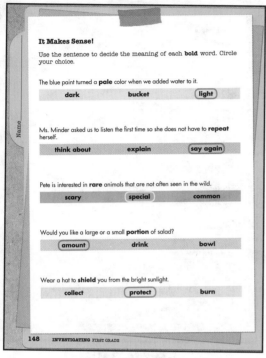

Page 148

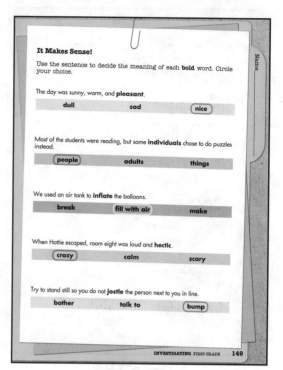

Page 149

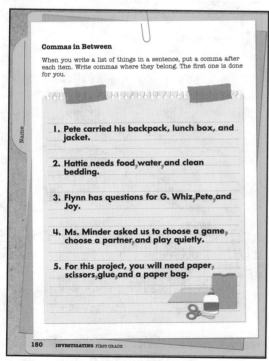

Page 150

Page 151

Great Dates

When you write a date, capitalize the name of the month. Write a comma between the number that tells the day and the number that tells the year. Look at important dates from Pete's life. Write each one correctly on the line.

Pete was born.
june 12 2009
June 12, 2009

Pete's family moved to a new town.
october 22 2010
October 22, 2010

Pete got a puppy.
december 25 2012
December 25, 2012

152 INVESTIGATING FIRST GRADE

Page 152

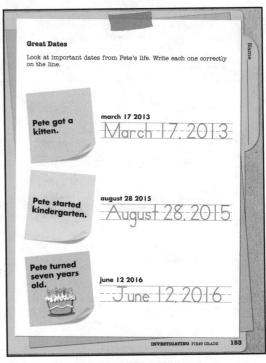

Great Dates

Look at important dates from Pete's life. Write each one correctly on the line.

Pete got a kitten.
march 17 2013
March 17, 2013

Pete started kindergarten.
august 28 2015
August 28, 2015

Pete turned seven years old.
june 12 2016
June 12, 2016

INVESTIGATING FIRST GRADE 153

Page 153

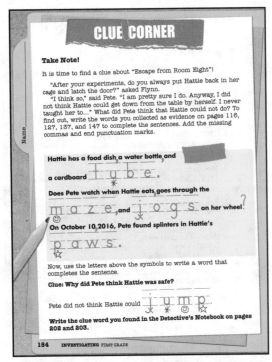

CLUE CORNER

Take Note!

It is time to find a clue about "Escape from Room Eight"!

"After your experiments, do you always put Hattie back in her cage and latch the door?" asked Flynn.

"I think so," said Pete. "I am pretty sure I do. Anyway, I did not think Hattie could get down from the table by herself. I never taught her to..." What did Pete think that Hattie could not do? To find out, write the words you collected as evidence on pages 116, 127, 137, and 147 to complete the sentences. Add the missing commas and end punctuation marks.

Hattie has a food dish a water bottle, and a cardboard **tube**.

Does Pete watch when Hattie eats, goes through the **maze**, and **jogs** on her wheel?

On October 10, 2016, Pete found splinters in Hattie's **paws**.

Now, use the letters above the symbols to write a word that completes the sentence.

Clue: Why did Pete think Hattie was safe?

Pete did not think Hattie could **jump**.

Write the clue word you found in the Detective's Notebook on pages 202 and 203.

154 INVESTIGATING FIRST GRADE

Page 154

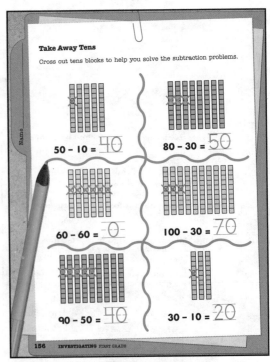

Take Away Tens

Cross out tens blocks to help you solve the subtraction problems.

50 − 10 = 40

80 − 30 = 50

60 − 60 = 0

100 − 30 = 70

90 − 50 = 40

30 − 10 = 20

156 INVESTIGATING FIRST GRADE

Page 156

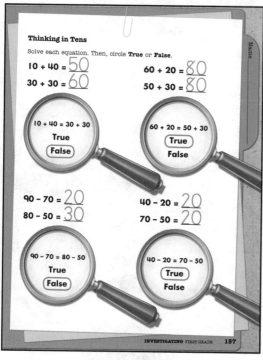

Page 157

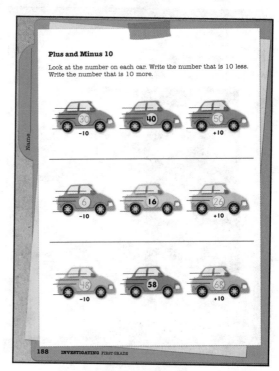

Page 158

Page 159

Page 160

ANSWER KEY

Page 161

Page 162

Page 163

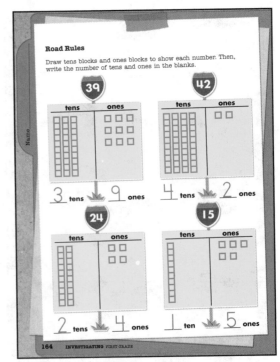

Page 164

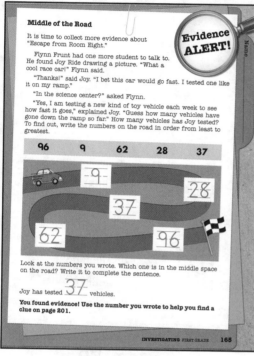

Page 165

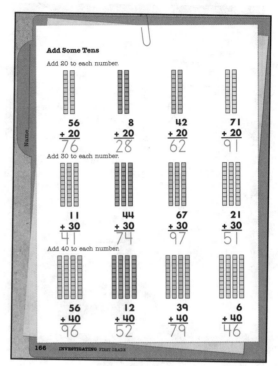

Page 166

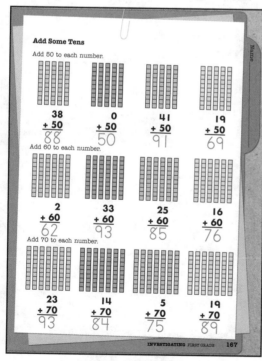

Page 167

Page 168

ANSWER KEY

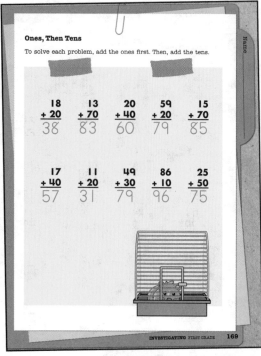

Page 169

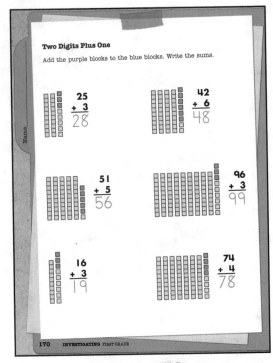

Page 170

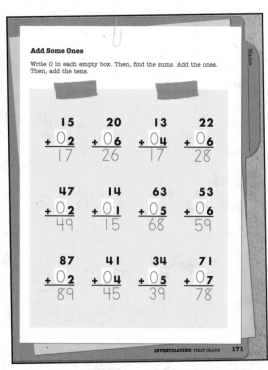

Page 171

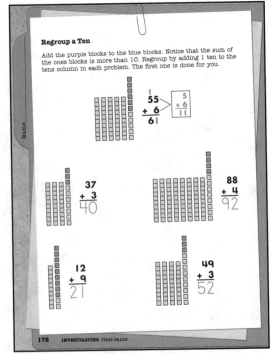

Page 172

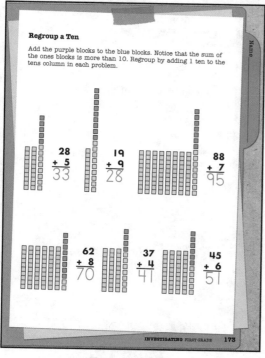

Page 173

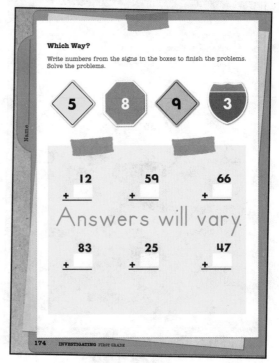

Page 174

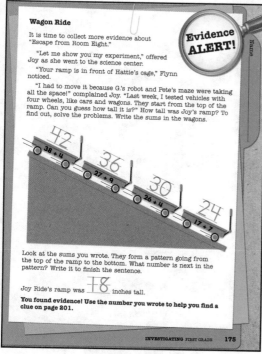

Page 175

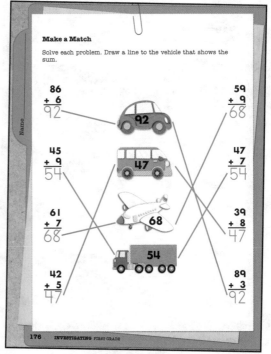

Page 176

ANSWER KEY

Page 177

Make a Match

Solve each problem. Draw a line to the vehicle that shows the sum.

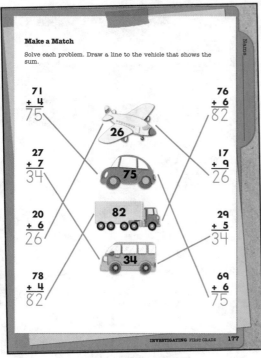

71 + 4 = 75

76 + 6 = 82

27 + 7 = 34

17 + 9 = 26

20 + 6 = 26

29 + 5 = 34

78 + 4 = 82

69 + 6 = 75

Vehicles: 26, 75, 82, 34

Page 177

Page 178

The Secret Number Is...

Solve the problems in each row. The number that all the sums share is the secret number. Write it in the blank.

The number in the tens place is ___.

49 + 3 = 52   51 + 4 = 55   45 + 5 = 50

The number in the ones place is _3_.

26 + 7 = 33   85 + 8 = 93   69 + 4 = 73

The number in the tens place is _9_.

87 + 3 = 90   93 + 6 = 99   85 + 7 = 92

Page 178

Page 179

The Secret Number Is...

Solve the problems in each row. The number that all the sums share is the secret number. Write it in the blank.

18 + 9 = 27   43 + 4 = 47   69 + 8 = 77

The number in the ones place is _7_.

36 + 5 = 41   44 + 4 = 48   33 + 7 = 40

The number in the tens place is _4_.

66 + 6 = 72   79 + 3 = 82   15 + 7 = 22

The number in the ones place is _2_.

Page 179

Page 180

What's the Problem?

Add or subtract.

80 − 50 = 30   31 + 20 = 51   45 + 6 = 51   90 − 30 = 60

73 + 10 = 83   89 + 4 = 93   60 + 25 = 85   70 − 40 = 30

14 + 80 = 94   60 − 10 = 50   67 + 9 = 76   46 + 3 = 49

Page 180

ANSWER KEY

Page 181

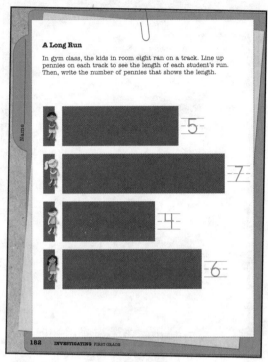

Page 182

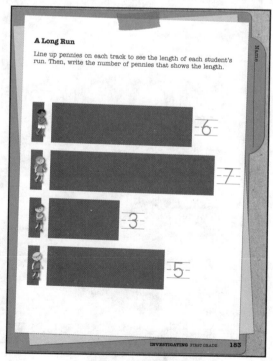

Page 183

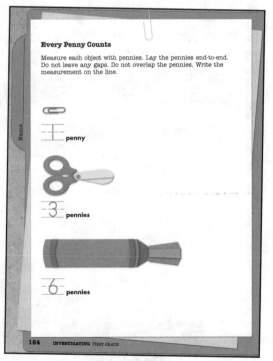

Page 184

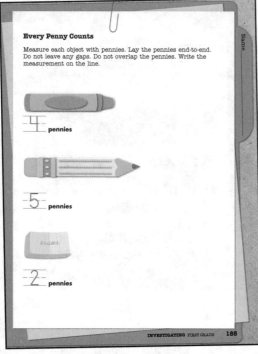

Page 185

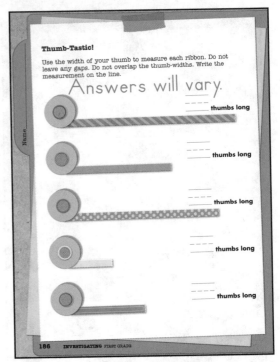

Page 186

Page 187

Page 188

Page 189

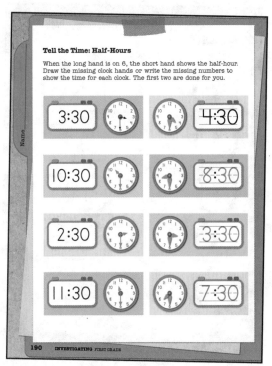

Page 190

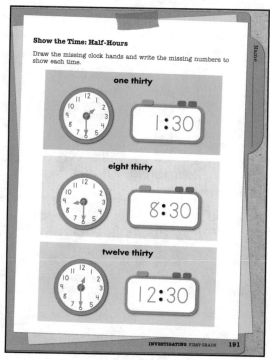

Page 191

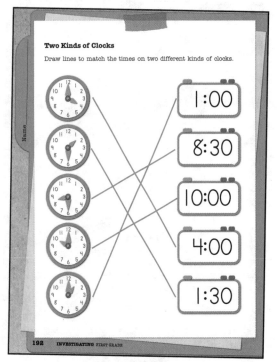

Page 192

ANSWER KEY

Page 193

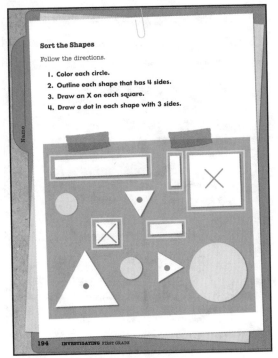

Page 194

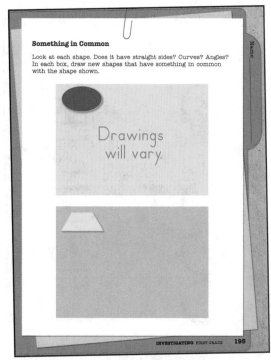

Page 195

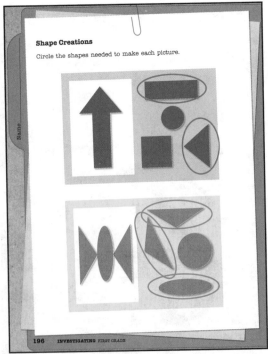

Page 196

ANSWER KEY

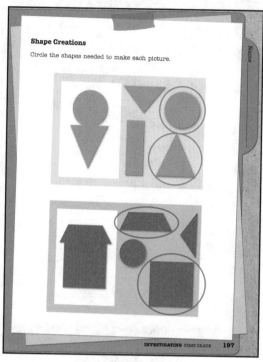

Page 197

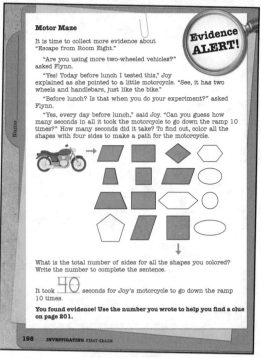

Page 198

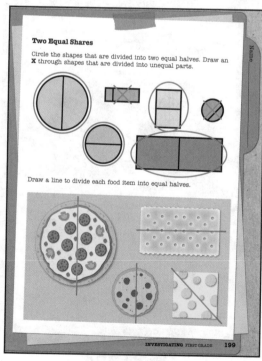

Page 199

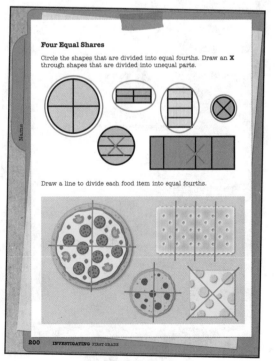

Page 200

Page 201

Page 202

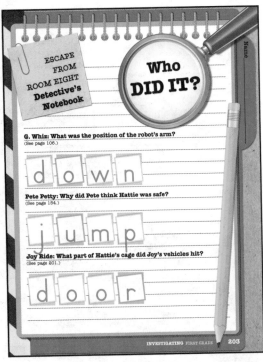

Page 203

Page 204

Page 205

"Someone or something must be opening the door from the outside," explained Flynn. "It could be Joy Ride. She moved her ramp in front of the cage. When motorcycles go down the ramp, they hit the door. The handlebars get stuck near the latch."

G. "That might be it," said Ms. Minder. "Do you have any other ideas?"

H. "Good work," said Ms. Minder. "That must be it! I will talk to Joy."

(I.) "It could not be Joy," said Ms. Minder. "Toy vehicles are not heavy enough to undo the latch."

"It could be Pete Petty," offered Flynn. "He may not latch the door when he puts Hattie back in her cage. He did not think she could jump down!"

L. "Good work," said Ms. Minder. "That must be it! I will talk to Pete."

M. "That might be it," said Ms. Minder. "Do you have any other ideas?"

(N.) "It could not be Pete," said Ms. Minder. "After he does experiments with Hattie, I make sure the cage door is latched. I will remind him that Hattie can jump!"

"It could be G. Whiz," tried Flynn. "His robot's timer makes the arm go down at one o'clock. That is right after recess! The robot is near the cage. Its arm could open the latch."

(O.) "Good work," said Ms. Minder. "That must be it! I did not know the robot had a timer."

P. "That might be it," said Ms. Minder. "Do you have any other ideas?"

Q. "It could not be G.," said Ms. Minder. "The timer is set for one o'clock in the morning, not one o'clock in the afternoon."

INVESTIGATING FIRST GRADE   **205**

Page 206

"We have another problem," said Flynn. "The science center is crowded. Kids cannot find space to work."

T. "I am afraid there is no more room," said Ms. Minder.

(U.) "Good point," said Ms. Minder. "We need another table in the science center. I will ask the principal to find one."

V. "Some students will have to put their projects away," said Ms. Minder.

"I am glad to hear that," said Flynn.

Q. "Hattie will be happier with more space," he said.

(R.) "Because I have an idea for a science project. By the way, do we have room for a guinea pig cage?" he asked.

S. "Maybe there will be room for Joy's cars, G.'s robot, and Hattie to race!" he joked.

"Hmm...we will see about that," said Ms. Minder. "I do know one thing. You are a clever investigator, Flynn Frunt. Thanks for solving the mystery in room eight!"

"You are welcome," said Flynn. "Let me know the next time there is a case to crack!"

206   INVESTIGATING FIRST GRADE

Congratulations

FIRST GRADE INVESTIGATOR!

You Solved the Case!

Escape from Room Eight

Science Center

FACTS: